THE
FORGIVENESS
OF
SINS

CHARLES WILLIAMS

WILLIAM B. EERDMANS
PUBLISHING COMPANY

GRAND RAPIDS
MICHIGAN

© 1942 Michael Williams

First published 1942 by Geoffrey Bles: The Centenary Press, London
This edition published 1984 by Wm. B. Eerdmans Publishing Co.
255 Jefferson Ave. S.E., Grand Rapids, MI 49503

Library of Congress Cataloging in Publication Data

Williams, Charles, 1886–1945.
The forgiveness of sins.

Reprint. Originally published: London : G. Bles, 1942.
1. Forgiveness of sin.   I. Title.
BT795.W55   1984   234'.5   84-12512

ISBN 0-8028-0032-7

CONTENTS

To

THE INKLINGS

I. INTRODUCTION

How is it possible to write a book on the Forgiveness of Sins? It is impossible. Great poets might do it, for they understand everything; and saints, for they are united with everything—creatures as well as Creator.

" I did pray all creatures," wrote Angela of Foligno, " (seeing how that I had offended them inasmuch as I had offended the Creator), that they would not accuse me before God. Then did it appear unto me that all creatures and all the saints did have compassion upon me, wherefore with a greater fire of love did I apply myself to praying unto God more than was customary."

The principles of the universe are clear to both those groups of sufferers. But other writers, who only repeat, more or less intelligently, with more or less goodwill, what they have been told; popularisers of the spirit whose duty is to the next moment; pedants and propagandists and other plagiarists of man's heart—what do we know about it? what can we say with any conviction, and with any style, of the crises of the spirit? We follow the fashion; the fashion, in our set, is to talk religion precisely as in other sets they talk films or finance. So we talk or we write; and, not having a high style to write in, not being able to manage words, we naturally persuade ourselves that colloquialisms and clichés are desirable. We must write for Everyman, and because it is reported that Everyman is crude, we must write crudely for him.

Yet if there is one thing which is obviously either a part of the universe or not—and on knowing whether it is or not our life depends—it is the forgiveness of sins. Our life depends on it in every sense. If there is God, if there is sin, if there is forgiveness, we must know it in order to live to him. If there are men, and if forgiveness is part of the interchanged life of men, then we must know it in order to live to and among them. Forgiveness, if it is at all a principle of that interchanged life, is certainly the deepest of all ; if it is not, then the whole principle of interchange is false. If the principle of retributive justice is our only hope we had certainly better know it. Because then, since retributive justice strictly existing everywhere is staringly impossible, all our hopes of interchange and union, of all kinds, are ended at once ; and we had better know *that*.

It is not however in this human discussion of the possibilities of forgiveness that the dark terror lies. We can happily universalise our individual experiences into theories there without feeling much horror, though not perhaps without doing some harm. The fear is in making statements about God. There both the possibility of truth and the possibility of communication fail. Neither rhetoric nor meiosis will serve ; the kingdom of heaven will not be defined by inexact terms, and exact terms. . . . Exact terms ! It is not altogether surprising that we are driven back sometimes on irony, even on a certain bitterness. At least, so, we acknowledge the impossibility of the task ; besides, we may find that our ironies are merely true. Irony is perhaps cheap but it is useful : it is (to use a metaphor itself ironic, cheap, and useful) a gas-mask against heaven. It is true we shall find we are carefully wearing it against pure air—that is the irony. But we should not at first have been able to bear the pure air without protection—that is the truth. It was the laughter of Beatrice in heaven which had once to be spared Dante—her laughter and heaven's song. The false smile of irony spares us for a while from the true smile of heaven.

All then that can really be hoped is that some semi-attentive reader, distrusting or despising what he reads, may turn from it to consider in himself the nature of forgiveness; so, and only so, can this consideration hope to be of any use. It is, as our Lord told us long ago, only the compulsion of the soul that leads to a true knowledge of the doctrine. It is true the comprehension of the blood beats with the same knowledge, though there not understood. Discussion and speculation are amusing enough; there are twenty-four hours in every day and they have to be got through somehow. Any fool can invent theories of the Fall, and when fools were interested in theology they frequently did; nowadays they are more concerned with economics or strategy or " ideals." Any fool can discuss how or what God, from his pure self-existence, knows, creates, or sustains. Even in reading the great doctors we sometimes become conscious of a sudden revolt, not perhaps in itself unwise. " The holy intellect," " our blessed reason "—we are like Wordsworth; we are bound to

> deem our blessed reason of least use
> Where wanted most.

The application of the finite to the infinite must surely

always be wrong ? Since we can never have all the
premises, how can our conclusions ever be true ?
Just ; yet the blood holds the need ; our physical
natures awake thought and even in some sense think ;
they measure good and evil after their kind. The
easy talk of mental distress being worse than physical
may occasionally be true ; only occasionally. Most
men would prefer a month's mental distress to a
month's serious neuralgia. It is in our bodies that
the secrets exist. Propitiation, expiation, forgiveness,
are maintained *there* when the mind has explained
them away—the need, and the means, and the fruition.

The secrets of extreme heaven and the secrets of
extreme earth are both obscure to us. It is between
these realities that explanation and diagram inade-
quately lie. The ways of approach are two. One
may begin by considering pardon as a fact in human
life, and so proceed to a meditation on its nature as a
divine act. Or one may begin by considering it as
a divine act and so conclude with the human. Discussions of human experience are nearly always unsatis-
factory. To ask " do we not all know ? " or " have
we not all felt ? " by the mere phrasing of the sentence
convinces the reader that he has neither known nor
felt. But some idea of pardon as men have known it is
necessary as a description if not as a definition. The
only safe place to find it is in those writers who have
been able to put it in undeniable phrases—especially
in the poets. I propose therefore first to examine how
forgiveness is presented in Shakespeare ; afterwards
how it appears in the theology of the Christian
Church ; and finally, how it operates, or should
operate, among men.

II. FORGIVENESS IN SHAKESPEARE

FORGIVENESS in Shakespeare is of three kinds, (i) the merely formal, (ii) the developed situation, as in *Measure for Measure*, (iii) the spontaneous reality in the last plays.   Over (i) no time need be spent.   As good an example as any is in the early *Two Gentlemen of Verona*. The play has to end, and the innocent hero and his outlaw associates have to be restored. The associates therefore are said to be " reformed," and the Duke generally forgives them all.   But we cannot take it at all seriously ; they are forgiven, as they were outlawed, for the convenience of the play, and for all the interest we have in them they might as well have been executed at once.   No one would have cared.   Much the same is true of the other earlier comedies ; whenever it is needed, there is always a reach-me-down forgiveness at hand. Shakespeare was not yet interested in what happens when men forgive. The most that can be said is that faults are overlooked : " all right, we won't say any more about it " is the general attitude.

(ii) A much more moving scene occurs during the last act of *Measure for Measure*. This is supposed to belong to the middle period of Shakespeare's career, after the early comedies and the histories and before the great tragedies. At this time Shakespeare was showing signs of going all "intellectual." He wrote several plays which might almost be called problem-plays—that is, they involved some kind of moral or philosophical question, though this was, of course, as was always Shakespeare's way, subordinated to the expression of the human heart. He did, in fact, abandon the intellectual method ; or perhaps it would be truer to say that he absorbed it into the other more inclusive method. *Troilus and Cressida*, which was written about this time, has a definite philosophical discussion of the nature of value ; it is the only thing of its kind in Shakespeare. *Measure for Measure* has nothing of that sort, but even *Measure for Measure* has a less normal plot than is customary with Shakespeare ; it is indeed almost ab-normal. It is the problem of a man naturally chaste, almost (could the phrase be allowed) naturally holy, though a little over-austere, tempted to lust and murder by the sight of a woman who is to him precisely a vision of chastity and sanctity. The situation is not, certainly, as abnormal as all that ; in our experiences sensuality and sanctity are so closely intertwined that our motives in some cases can hardly be separated until the tares are gathered out of the wheat by heavenly wit. The tale of the play is known well enough. Angelo is chaste, and being made governor of Verona instead of the Duke who pretends to go on a journey, condemns a young man named Claudio to death (according to the law) for having intercourse with a girl, before marriage. Isabella, Claudio's sister, a novice of St. Clare, appeals to the Deputy for her brother's pardon. He falls in love with her, and offers her the pardon in exchange for her consent to his lust.

> O cunning enemy, that to catch a saint
> With saints dost bait thy hook !

There is no need to digress into further coils.   By a

trick his earlier pledged love Mariana is substituted for
Isabella. But when the night is ended Angelo orders
Claudio to be executed. The Duke returns and all the
evil is brought to light.

It is now that the scene of pardon opens. It is not
perhaps composed, except here and there, of great
poetry; but we are not here concerned with it as
poetry, but with the diagram that is expressed in the
poetry. Angelo himself, when all is discovered, begs
for punishment.

> Then, good prince,
> No longer session hold upon my shame,
> But let my trial be my own confession.
> Immediate sentence then and sequent death
> Is all the grace I beg.

The Duke condemns him. But Mariana pleads for his
pardon, and in her anguish begs Isabella to plead with
her. The Duke protests that such a request is
"against all sense." Mariana continues to invoke
Isabella: and at the very last moment Isabella,
realising fully that Angelo has meant to seduce her
and kill her brother (and supposing he has certainly
done the last), suddenly yields. She kneels before
the Duke; in a grave and very moving line, she
begins:

> Most bounteous sir,
> Look, if it please you, on this man condemned. . . .

She intercedes; she says all that can be said on his
behalf; she asks for his pardon. The play moves
on to its end, but that moment has been seized by
the way.

What is of interest here is that, by chance or by

choice, Shakespeare allows the two persons between
whom the wrong existed to make to the Duke two
opposed requests. He who has caused the wrong
asks for his punishment ; she who has suffered it asks
for his pardon. I am always reluctant to draw from
the plays any deductions, except in the most general
terms, about Shakespeare's personal opinions ; and
I do not suggest that we have any right to be shocked,
after this scene, when we find Shakespeare claiming
payment of debts due to him in the law-courts. Nor,
on the other hand, ought we to neglect this poetic
moment because of Shakespeare's personal behaviour.
It may be but an accident of the conclusion of the play.
But it is an intense and exciting accident, and its
excitement and intensity depend on the greatness of
the wrong done to Isabella, on her pause before she
consents to ask the Duke to forgive, and on the
reciprocal attitude of the two concerned. We recognise the power of the idea.

(iii) In the tragedies the question of forgiveness does
not arise. It may be said that that is one reason why
they are tragedies. The hesitation to regard oneself as
wronged, the capacity not to brood over wrong—
this itself is lacking in Hamlet and Othello. It is a
personal grudge, indulged, which distracts both of
them. The wrongs of Lear are lost in madness ; the
sins of Macbeth are offered no chance of pardon.
That is the nature of those plays. But in the last
comedies something else enters at the end—pardon
certainly, but no longer the serious and considered
pardon of *Measure for Measure*. Now pardon has
no longer to compel itself to move ; it moves at once ;
it runs. It is again to be allowed that this is the

solution which the different style of those last plays demanded. But at least the imagination of Shakespeare was able to discover such a solution. In *Measure for Measure* pardon had been a delayed and virtuous determination of Isabella's chaste and devoted mind. But in *Cymbeline* it is so swift that it seems almost to create the love to which it responds. The noblest of Shakespeare's women, Imogen, has been condemned by her husband Posthumus to death for (as he thinks) disloyalty. She supposes him to be in love with someone else, and to desire her death, and she rebukes him to herself with the phrase :

> My dear lord,
> Thou art one of the false ones.

It is the tenderest reproach in literature. But in the last act she does not wait for him to ask her forgiveness ; the word is not named. It is true that he has in fact already repented of his intention to have her killed, though he still believes her guilty. But the supposed murder lies heavy on him and, solitary and in prison, he broods upon it. He also desires to die on her account, though he does not think the gods, " more clement than vile men," desire it. His repentance is by them " desired more than constrained." The gods made his life, and therefore (and only therefore) it may be weighed equal with Imogen's. He has a passion for repentance, and perhaps it is this yielding of his life which is, to himself, the only exposition of repentance. He is so far worthy of and prepared for her forgiveness. But the real difference is in the resentment and the lack of resentment with which they separately feel the original offence, real or supposed.

In the final crisis she turns to him with a cry of protest-in-love and of renewal-in-love :

> Why did you throw your wedded lady from you ?
> Think that you are upon a rock, and now
> Throw me again.

She can even make a play upon the word " throw " in her high delight; and Posthumus can only accept the beauty with a renewed fidelity. It is true that they are in a special relationship of love ; the other pardons in the play are of a more distant kind and have to be more formally expressed. The last act of *Cymbeline*, let it be admitted, is a wild dance of melodramatic recognitions and long-lost children with strawberry-marks. But the style of Imogen is the keynote of all ; the pardon of Imogen the pattern of all ; and both style and pardon, though so heavenly, are as realistic as anything in Shakespeare. Her father says of her that she looks at those present, hitting

> each object with a joy ; the counterchange
> Is severally in all.

As if in that " counterchange of joy " Posthumus says to his enemy—but this time after an expressed grief :

> Kneel not to me.
> The power that I have on you is to spare you,
> The malice, to forgive.

And the king follows with :

> Pardon's the word to all.

The thought is even carried on into the final—and political—settlement. The king has conquered the Romans, but he then proposes to submit and pay the tribute, the refusal of which had been the occasion of the war. There is, in this sense, a peculiar fitness in the departure of the persons of the play to the temple of Jupiter:

> Let's smoke the temple with our sacrifices.

Such a departure is, certainly, a dramatic expedient for getting them off the stage, and it is not accompanied by any great lines of verse; it need not therefore be taken too carefully. Still, for what it is worth, it is there; and it is worth precisely *that* choice of departure instead of any other—feasts or weddings or what not.

The theme of pardon is therefore more expressed in *Cymbeline* than in the other two late comedies. It may be repeated that no deduction can be made from the plays concerning Shakespeare's personal life. He may or he may not have wished, or indeed been able, to forgive those (if any) who had injured him as he imagined Imogen forgiving. But at least he understood such a forgiveness; and took a poetic advantage of it. The carelessness of style he pretended to show in those last plays—as if the most wonderful phrases fell from him by chance—is the full maturity of style: *ars celare artem*—it was his lordliest art to pretend that his art was nothing. And this too is, artistically, the cause of his phrasing of the speed of pardon; he would not have it heavy. But the realistic style reflects a realism: this is what the loveliest pardon is—it is love renewing itself in a mutual and exchanged knowledge.

In the other two late comedies the nature of pardon is not so definitely expressed: its speed and reality is

left to the fact that nothing is said, or hardly anything.
In the *Winter's Tale* the only phrase is

> Both your pardons
> That ere I put between your holy looks
> My ill suspicion.

The reconciliations accept this and seem courteously
to set it aside, but they do not verbally comment on it.
The comment they imply is given in Prospero's
speech in the *Tempest*. There one of the wrongdoers
exclaims :

> O how odd 'twill sound that I
> Must ask my child forgiveness ;

and Prospero answers :

> There, sir, stop.
> Let us not burden our remembrance with
> A heaviness that's gone.

This answer comes somewhere between Isabella's
deliberateness and Imogen's speed : it has a grave joy
of its own, but that joy consists in forgetting rather
than in recollecting the past. These two methods
are the double technique of pardon ; we shall have
occasion to consider them both presently.

It has seemed worth while recalling these Shakespearean moments for several reasons. They are
the infinite statement of a certain human experience
without reference to anything but itself. They are
the finest expressions of that experience in English
verse. And they include various types, or (say)
methods of pardon. There is the deliberate—and
(in the play) it is to be supposed religious—act of
Isabella ; pardon corresponding to penitence, and
penitence demanding penalty as pardon offers free-

dom : a union of passions, but a grave and deliberate union. Such was the power of Shakespeare's middle style : he reached the deep human experiences by a noble sound of approach ; there is a kind of ceremony in the verse—" Most bounteous sir. . . ." But after that, and after the tragedies, he reached a new kind of style, and took full advantage of it. Love was never so much mere love ; death never so much mere death ; jealousy never so much mere jealousy ; pardon never so much mere pardon as there.

I do not deny that this high realisation of pardon may have derived from the Christian religion. But we must not say that Shakespeare showed it as so deriving. It is clear that he gave it to personages in whom he implied no touch of what the theologians call grace. I am aware that he used the word a number of times, and off and on. But no one has yet, I think, tried to prove that Imogen was a devout Christian woman. It is her glory that she is purely natural ; it is her double glory that her nature holds within it a state of being equivalent, one might say, to sanctity. Further than that glorious youth— beautiful, frank, fierce, and direct—Shakespeare had no opportunity to pursue her, for the play had an end, and Imogen. But if a fancy might be permitted, it would be that the old age of Imogen was as wise as her youth, and her power of lucid pardon never slothful ; that " all her acts," in the phrase with which Florizel in the *Winter's Tale* praised Perdita—" all her acts were queens." It is towards that state of being that forgiveness aims ; the sufficiency of the actions of the soul need this virtue as their condition.

There are, of course, other poets in whom the

theme of forgiveness appears ; not, perhaps, so many.
It is not, I think, actually in Shelley, for all his lyric
song about the disappearance of evil ; at least, the
difficulty of it is not there.   It is in Milton, as it is in
Dante, but in both it is, or is meant to be, a Christian
pardon, and it will be more convenient to discuss that
directly in its own nature rather than indirectly in
them.   It is certainly in Blake, and he may enter
presently as a comment on the theme ; it is in Brown-
ing's *Ring and the Book*, and in that poem Pompilia
again casts the word aside—

> I—pardon him ? . . .
>   I am saved through him,
> So as by fire ; to him, thanks and farewell.

It is not, I think, much in later poets, who are
concerned more with the agony than the solution,
with ironic or tragic themes rather than with those of
comedy.   But forgiveness is the resolution of all into
a kind of comedy, the happiness of reconciliation, the
peace of love.

III. THE SIN OF ADAM

This then is the Shakespearean statement of pardon, and it is put forward here as a high presentation of human experience. It is not especially religious in spite of the semi-religious setting, though it is certainly capable of a profound religious interpretation. But it does not, to all readers, necessarily involve that ; it can be, for atheists as well as Christians, a maxim of the normal human intelligence. This, one way or another, whatever else it may be, whatever the cause may be, is what forgiveness between men must be. It remains to consider it in relation to the particular Christian pattern of the universe.

The beginning of all this specific creation was the Will of God to incarnate.[1] God himself is pure spirit ; that is, in so far as any defining human word can apply to him, he is pure spirit. He had created matter, and he had determined to unite himself with matter. The means of that union was the Incarnation : that is, it was determined that the Word was to be flesh and to be man.

It is clear that this, like all his other acts, might have been done to himself alone. It was certainly not necessary for him to create man in order that he might himself become man. The Incarnation did not involve the Creation. But it was within his

[1] It will be obvious from what follows that I am here following one arrangement of doctrine rather than what is perhaps the more usual. But I am instructed that it is no less orthodox.

Nature to will to create joy, and he willed to create
joy in this manner also.

He willed therefore that his union with matter in
flesh should be by a mode which precisely involved
creatures to experience joy. He determined to be
incarnate by being born ; that is, he determined to
have a mother. His mother was to have companions
of her own kind ; and the mother and her companions
were to exist in an order of their own degree, in time
and place, in a world. They were to be related to
him and to each other by a state of joyous knowledge ; they were to derive from him and from each
other ; and he was to deign to derive his flesh from
them. All this sprang, superfluous, out of his original
intention—superfluous to himself and his direct
purpose, not superfluous to his indirect purpose of
love. It was to be a web of simultaneous interchange
of good. "In the sight of God," said the Lady
Julian, " all man is one man and one man is all man."

This high creation came into existence ; we have
now the shadows, hints, and fractions of it for our
instruction and encouragement. And that is all we
have, except for the new work which was presently
to follow. The original shone, in its proper glory,
aware of its nature and of the nature of its lord. We
cannot now make much of a guess at its nature, nor
whether (for example) it was sequential in our
sense ; whether the Divine Birth was, in that state,
in existence or still to be. The creation must
presumably have been related to time in order that
derivation (as between children and parents) should
take place at all. But whether its only consciousness
was of what we may call " time " may be doubted ;

simultaneity may also have been known. To know simultaneity is not, of itself, to know eternity ; that is a different matter altogether.

Its occasion, root, and centre was the Incarnation ; that was the cause of it and the reason for it. The operation of the Holy Ghost was at once over the world and in the womb. It was a free generosity of love that deigned to create both the world and the secret womb ; neither were necessary to his existence in flesh. But it was a generosity which perfectly foresaw (to talk in terms of time) the future, both for himself and for his creation. It would perhaps be more accurate to say that all was certainly then present to him, as it presumably could not be to the creation. But one cannot talk of it in those terms. It is our first intellectual descent from heaven ; we are compelled to use terms which we know are inaccurate. St. Paul gave us a new vocabulary, and the great doctors have continued the work. Theology, like all sciences, has its own proper language, but even the theologians are always sliding back into a one-sided use of that language. Their terms ought to be ambiguous ; they ought to carry meanings at once in time and outside time. It cannot be done ; and if it cannot among those experts, it certainly cannot among lesser creatures. So one is compelled to talk of God foreseeing and God determining, of pure Act as divisible, of eternity as altering, of perfection as becoming.

It is therefore that we are driven to speak of the Creation and the Redemption as separate acts and even separate ideas ; as if Bridges's phrase of " a divine fiasco " was obscurely justified. Even so intelligent

a mind failed to grasp the very conditions of thought
upon such things,

For I reckon it among the unimaginables//how St. Thomas,
with all his honesty and keen thought . . .//should with
open eyes have accepted for main premiss//the myth of a
divine fiasco, on which to assure//the wisdom of God : leading
to a foregone conclusion//of illachrymable logic.

But certainly alteration there was.   The possibility
of alteration had been created as an element in the
whole. That web of diagrammatised glory, of honour-
able beauty, of changing and interchanging adoration,
depended for its perfection on two things—the will
of God to sustain its being and its own will to be so
sustained. He made—if we call it obedience we
make the joy too dull (since we have, except at our
momentary best and in our transient illuminations,
lost the joy of obedience) ; he made—let us say the
delight of a perfect response to his initiative a part of
the working of the web. We could not otherwise
become at once perfect servitude and perfect freedom.
They are one and interchangeable, at least in consciousness : even now, in some states of love, it is
possible at once to delight in being bound and to
delight in being free. As Blake said : " Contraries
are not negations." Much less there. In this world
they tend to become opposites ; that too perhaps is
the result of what then happened.

But what did happen ? The web depended on its
exchanged derivation, which itself sprang from the
fact not only that all derived from him but also that
he had ordained that he, in his flesh, would derive
from all. The two derivations were, in him, a single
act ; and in that act, free and yet bound, bound by its

free choice, all lay.   Somewhere, somehow, the web
loosed itself from its centre—also by its free choice.
It chose ; and it chose, in our phrase, wrongfully.
What and how it chose we do not know.   It may have
been, literally, greed—some silly thing like a fruit ;
our own experience shows us how often the greatest
spiritual decisions depend on something almost
equally trivial—money or sexual pleasure.   It may
have been some other silly thing like pride—say,
the belief that it could and would produce the
divine Child of its own energy, an intoxication with
its own powers, a worship of its own self.   It may
have been in this sense a dark mystery precisely of the
birth of Christ.

But also it may have been what it is described as
being in the old myth of Genesis.   I may perhaps be
permitted to quote here what I have written elsewhere
of that great myth :

" The nature of the Fall—both while possible and
when actual—is clearly defined.   The ' fruit of the
tree ' is to bring an increase of knowledge.   That
increase, however, is, and is desired as being, of a
particular kind.   It is not merely to know more, but
to know in another method.   It is primarily the
advance (if it can be so called) from knowing good
to knowing good and evil ; it is (secondarily) the
knowing " as gods."   A certain knowledge was, by
its nature, confined to divine beings.   Its communication to man would be, by its nature, disastrous to
man.   The Adam had been created and were existing
in a state of knowledge of good and nothing but good.
They knew that there was some kind of alternative,
and they knew that the rejection of the alternative

was part of their relation to the Omnipotence that
created them. That relation was part of the good
they enjoyed. But they knew also that the knowledge
in the Omnipotence was greater than their own ;
they understood that in some way it knew ' evil.'

"It was, in future ages, declared by Aquinas that it
was of the nature of God to know all possibilities, and
to determine which possibility should become fact.
' God would not know good things perfectly, unless
he also knew evil things . . . for, since evil is not of
itself knowable, forasmuch as " evil is the privation
of good," as Augustine says (*Confess*. iii. 7), therefore
evil can neither be defined nor known except by good.'
Things which are not and never will be he knows
' not by vision,' as he does all things that are, or will
be, ' but by simple intelligence.' It is therefore part
of that knowledge that he should understand good in
its deprivation, the identity of heaven in its opposite
identity of hell, but without ' approbation,' without
calling it into being at all.

"It was not so possible for man, and the myth is the
tale of that impossibility. However solemn and
intellectual the exposition of the act sounds, the act
itself is simple enough. It is easy for us now, after
the terrible and prolonged habit of mankind ; it was
not, perhaps, very difficult then—as easy as picking a
fruit from a tree. It was merely to wish to know an
antagonism in the good, to find out what the good
would be like if a contradiction were introduced into
it. Man desired to know schism in the universe.
It was a knowledge reserved to God ; man had been
warned that he could not bear it—" in the day that
thou eatest thereof thou shalt surely die.' A serpen-

tine subtlety overwhelmed that statement with a grander promise—' Ye shall be as gods, knowing good and evil.' Unfortunately to be as gods meant, for the Adam, to die, for to know evil, for them, was to know it not by pure intelligence but by experience. It was, precisely, to experience the opposite of good, that is the deprivation of the good, the slow destruction of the good, and of themselves with the good.

" The Adam were permitted to achieve this knowledge if they wished; they did so wish. Some possibility of opposite action there must be if there is to be any relation between different wills. Free-will is a thing incomprehensible to the logical mind, and perhaps not very often possible to the human spirit. The glasses of water which we are so often assured that we can or can not drink do not really refract light on the problem. ' *Nihil sumus nisi voluntates*,' said Augustine, but the thing we fundamentally are is not easily known. Will is rather a thing we may choose to become than a thing we already possess—except so far as we can a little choose to choose, a little will to will. The Adam, with more will, exercised will in the myth. They knew good; they wished to know good and evil. Since there was not—since there never has been and never will be—anything else than the good to know, they knew good as antagonism. All difference consists in the mode of knowledge. They had what they wanted. That they did not like it when they got it does not alter the fact that they certainly got it."

So much for the actual choice in itself. But the making of that choice may have been single or multitudinous. We know so little of that high state which

haunts us for ever in our exile, and makes that exile
preferable to us, and terrifies rather than encourages
us with the hope of our return; it is not in mortal
affairs alone that we can speak of " hope that is
unwilling to be fed "—we know so little of it that its
conditions are unimaginable. But I have wondered
if indeed we were not all there, if all mankind was not
then simultaneous and co-inherent, and whether all
mankind did not then choose amiss. It would not,
in fact, be more astonishing than that one should ; or
the choice of one may, in fact, have wrecked all.
But Adam may have been our name as well as our
single father's, we in him and he in us in a state other
than sequence. We were in him for we were he.
We were all there, and we were all greedy or proud or
curious. The original sin was in us as we originally
were. The co-inherent will of mankind moved, and
moved against its divine Original, which is the
definition, so far, of sin.

Either then, we, ourselves, were in that state and
there chose indeed [1] ; or—and this has been the more
common doctrine in the Church—the state of man's
co-inherence was then so intense that the whole
original body was desperately affected by the act of
its primal member. The description of the new
creation in the Epistle to the Ephesians is, reversed,
a description of the Fall : " that we . . . may grow
up into him in all things, which is the head, even
Christ : From whom the whole body fitly joined
together and compacted by that which every joint
supplieth, according to the effectual working in the

---

[1] I do not mean to involve a pre-natal existence. The choice is of
another kind.

measure of every part, maketh increase of the body
unto the edifying of itself in love." " That we may
grow away from him in all things . . . the whole
body disjoined and decompacted . . . decreases . . ."
—The body was dissolved, or dissolved as far as
could be, by the too-effectual working of that which
every joint supplied.

The word " body " there was not only meta-
phorical. The principle of the Incarnation had been
a unity of God and Man in the flesh ; and the principle
of the creation had therefore been a unity of man—
soul and body—in flesh. The physical body
belonged to the category of the virtues, as everything
did. We have, except for the poets, rather lost this
sense of the body ; we have not only despised it too
much, but we have not admired it enough. There is a
phrase in Wordsworth's *Prelude* (Book VIII., ll.
279–81) which defines it. Speaking of the Shepherds
whom he has seen among the hills, he says :

> The human form
> To me became an index of delight,
> Of grace and honour, power and worthiness.

The operative word there is *index*. The body is
there seen as an index to those holy qualities which we
call Virtues. It is true we have largely lost the
capacity of understanding the references in the index ;
in the whole great volume of our nature we do not
know to which page the entries in the index, the
references in the body, properly allude. We can
remark sometimes in the love-poets something of the
same sort, as when Dante talks in the *Convivio* of the
mouth of the Lady of the Window, or Shakespeare

of how love accentuates " the functions and the
offices " of the body, or Patmore says that in the
body

> Every least part
> Astonish'd hears
> And sweet replies to some like region of the spheres.

But we do not all of us take the love-poets seriously.
Wordsworth however was not (in that particular
sense) in love with the Shepherds, and it is he who
uses the word *index*.   I do not propose here to discuss
the whole matter ; it must be sufficient to say that on
this interpretation the body is in one category what the
soul is in another.   The Lady Julian of Norwich said
that : " In the self-same point that our soul is made
sensual, in the self-same point is the City of God
ordained to him from without beginning "—a not
dissimilar maxim.   The body was made as the
physical formula of the Virtues, and whenever our
eyes are opened we clearly perceive it to be so.

But then the chief name of all that balance and interchange and union of the Virtues in flesh was Chastity ;
for Chastity was precisely the name of its union with
the Incarnation.   Monks or married people, hermits
or lovers, had this rule in whatever variation because
of that union.   Chastity is the obedience to and the
relation with the adorable central body.   It usually
sounds to us now (let it be admitted) something of a
negative virtue.   That is false.   It is the result of the
Fall, after which, in the process of knowing good as
evil, all virtues were bound, both in their physical and
spiritual categories, to be understood rather by their
positive denials than by their positive affirmations :
even sometimes by their vicious opposites rather than

by themselves. To suffer the Fall in this sense is
what we had, and have, to expect. " But in the beginning it was not so." " It is usual to interpret this
' beginning ' as a matter of temporal succession and
to see no more in it than an indication of the order of
sequence of events. . . . This ' beginning ' imports
rather a divine principle of life." [1] The principle of
the relation of the created nature towards the Creator
in that beginning is named Chastity ; it is the natural
relation in the beginning and the supernatural now.
The imagination of this is what fills the word ; it is
not our quiet and chilling fancies that should limit it.
The glory of the Divine Word itself is its chastity ;
the glory of the word " chastity " is the reflection of
the Divine Word. We have been taught that it is
the principle of what we mean by celestial immortality ;
which is union with the Word in terms of everlasting-
ness as " eternity" is union in the terms of uncreated
simultaneity. Milton, in *Comus*, defined it so for all
English verse and for all English attention, though
indeed attention is the last thing we have given to the
great speech of the Elder Brother, in that masque and
ballet of "divine philosophy." [2] There he speaks of
chastity as that quality which immortalises the flesh.
But the phrase—

> turns it by degrees to the soul's essence
> Till all be made immortal——

[1] Sergius Bulgakov : *The Wisdom of God.* I am not here claiming
more agreement with the book than the quotation implies. " The
position is familiar," but I do not remember to have seen it so clearly
asserted before.

[2] It has been pointed out to me that the masque usually involved a
dance, and that Milton for the actual dance substituted a philosophical.
The suggestion is so much in accord with the high gaiety of *Comus* that
I wish I had thought of it myself. The physical nature of the dance
passes into the intellectual measure and there maintains itself in the sound
of the verse.

implies perhaps too much alteration on the part of
the holy flesh which was dragged down with the will
but which was not itself the origin of the Fall, since
initiative could only act by the assent of the will.

Chastity then is part of that charity which (we have
been taught) is the fulfilling of the law.   It is the love
of the soul for God.   The other part of that charity
is courtesy, which is the love of the soul for its created
companions.   " On these two commandments hang
all the law and the prophets."   They are comple-
mentary ;   nay, they are one.   Chastity is courtesy
towards God ;   courtesy is chastity towards men.
The practice of the single virtue is named differently
only in order that we may the more adequately enter
into those divine secrets which it is our business to
restore.   It is this single virtue which was lost by the
Fall ;   or say the two were lost—chastity and courtesy.
They were lost in both body and soul, and the breach
between body and soul, the breach in the indivisible,
was fully established.   The great physical ratification
of that breach was Death.   Whether something like
Death—some change, some conversion—existed
before the Fall we cannot know.   But the Bible is
full of suggestions that Death, as we do know it, is
a result of the Fall.   It is an outrage ;   it is a necessary
outrage.   It is a schism between those two great
categories of physical and spiritual which formed the
declaration in unity of one identity.   Sin had come
into the great co-inherent web of humanity ;   say
rather that all the web burst into sin, and broke or was
antagonised within itself ;   knot against knot, and
each filament everywhere countercharged within
itself.   It broke ? alas, no ;   it could not break unless

its maker consented that it should and he would not consent; his goodwill towards it (we are assured) was too great. He loved it; he had loved it in the making and loved it made; and like any mortal lover he would not consent that his wife should cease to love him. He would not consent that she should go; that is, as between him and her, that she should cease to exist; that is, in this only case, that she should absolutely cease to exist. Death, and the second death, might be the result; he was not to be moved. No; she had turned from him; she had attempted to deracinate her life; but he was still her root, and she should still have at her disposal all that he had given her; she should still have life. Intolerable charity!

Sin then had come in. But what then is sin? It is easier to talk about, to preach about, to rebuke, perhaps even to repent, than to understand. Man had in some way determined to be greedy or curious or proud, and this was an " offence " to God. The grand web had wished to know evil and it did. But in what sense could this be an " offence " to its Creator? Is the Lord more like our fallen selves than we had supposed? Is he also proud and greedy, and therefore in the worst sense jealous? Envious, by definition, he can hardly be. But can that divine Other be credited even with our virtues? We are continuously asked by the little books to consider, for example, how horrible gluttony and fornication are to the " holiness " of the Lord. We are to look at " God's awful purity "; and when at any rate we look at the phrase, it seems completely meaningless. How can God be " pure "? How can our lascivious-

ness kindle, as we are told it does, his "wrath"?
I have spoken above of the "generosity" of love;
but again, strictly considered, how can Omnipotence
be generous or Omniscience wise? He laid commandments on us; we disobey; very well, is he to
be angry? Obviously not, unless he chooses that he
shall; all his motions are his will. If one created
(if one could and dared) two blackbeetles, and bade
them copulate only on Tuesdays and they did it on
Thursday, would one be "angry" with them unless
one chose? Make the command as rational as one
can; suppose one had made them only capable of
happy copulation once in seven days, and they hurt
themselves by disobedience—even then, would one
be *angry*? Still less, he; unless indeed it is supposed
to be part of his nature to permit himself the infinite
indulgence of superior spite.

But it will be said that nowadays we do not think
in those terms. It is not God who is "angry"; it
is we who have set ourselves in such a relation to him
that we can only know him as a fire and a hostility.
The Judgement has been reduced from a supernatural to a natural thing; it is the moral law within
and not the moral law without which is our test.
Certainly if the first sin were to know good as evil
then this is credible, for it is precisely knowing our
own good as evil. If men were determined to know
that, then it was that which they must know. So to
abolish the spectacular Judgement, however, does not
help much. "It is he who made us, and not we
ourselves." The awful responsibility of the First
Cause remains with the First Cause. The great St.
Thomas laid down that since God's dignity is infinite,

therefore an offence against it must be infinite in guilt,
and demand infinite punishment. But part of that
infinite dignity was to create and sustain ; he sustains
therefore in hell that he may so avenge himself ?
Supernatural judgement or natural sequence, we return
to the single cry that goes up against the Creator ; it
is but one variation on one theme : that he did create,
that he was the First Cause.

Yes : but that creation had been after a particular
manner. That act which is called the Fall was an act
by a being who had not (in a sense) only been created.
He *had* been created, of course, but according to a
special order which involved the non-created. He
was " in flesh," or rather he was flesh at least as much
as anything else. He was the only rational creature
so made, and his flesh was in unique relationship to
the sublime flesh which was the unity of God with
matter. The Incarnation was the single dominating
fact, and to that all flesh was related. The self-
communicated Joy of that was to be an all-commun-
cated joy. It was related to all. The Fall therefore
was not an affair which would necessarily leave the
central and glorious Body unaffected. The angels
were different. They might rebel and their rebellion
be only in relation to God as Creator. In that sense,
spirit as they might be, those celestial and splendid
beings were wholly different from their Maker. But
on earth it was not so. The Incarnation was the
Original from which the lesser living human images
derived. It was to be, if it was not already, intimately
connected with their flesh ; for it was to derive—
since he had so decreed—from their flesh ; if indeed
it did not already in their simultaneity so derive. He

had determined to be born of a mother, and that she also should be born of hers; and that physical relations of blood should unite him with all men and women that were or were to be. The Fall therefore took place in a nature which was as close as that to his own incarnate Nature.

To talk of God being in a dilemma is not only heretical but flagrantly silly : God is not like that. But it may perhaps be said that, when he created those superfluous beings of joy, he knew what they would do for to his eternity they were already doing it. He might, therefore, to borrow a word from the Old Testament writers, have " repented himself "—had he allowed himself repentance. He might have abolished mankind. It had had its moment, its chance of co-inherent glory; it had refused it; let it go. Actually he " might " not because he did not. But let the imbecile phrase stand; it does at least express the dilemma in which our understanding is placed. He might, but he did not. He might have abolished mankind and still, uniquely, have been flesh ; he might indeed have been flesh through the uniquely preserved immaculacy of his mother alone, or with such others of her companions as he predestinated to be saved from that falling co-inherence into a sustained co-inherence with his mother and with himself. He did not. He preserved his original purpose, as he had known, from the beginning, he would.

What then ? This was the intolerable charity of which we are speaking. Mankind had devoted itself to an egotism which meant destruction, incoherence, and hell. He would not let it cease to exist. But then the result was that if he was to submit to the

choice of man, he was indeed to submit to that choice.
He was not merely to put up with it as a Creator, he
was to endure it as a Victim. Whatever sin was, it
was a thing repugnant to his nature as Man, repugnant
to his flesh ; that was, in fact, its definition. Whether
it was greed or pride or envy, it was still that which
the Divine Word, in the limits he desired to set upon
his earthly existence, would not permit himself to
will. He derived, in his flesh, from men and women ;
but also in that Incarnation he derived from his Father
wholly and from his Father's will. Man had chosen
an opposite behaviour. Greed or envy or pride, it
was opposed to the nature and movement—yes, even
the physical movement—of God in flesh. God in
flesh was to maintain both incarnation and creation ;
he must then be the Victim of the choice of man.
But why maintain it ? there is but one answer—for
love. Intolerable charity indeed—but now also
intolerable for himself. Indeed, it killed him.

It is this love which has been the continual astonish-
ment of Christianity, to others and to itself. It is this
capacity and will in himself—in himself absolutely—
of love towards his superfluous creatures which has
seemed strange and adorable to that creation so thrown
" out of the pale of love." But the pale itself is
adoration, and wherever adoration exists the pale of
love is recovered. It is everywhere strange also,
within or without the pale, but the strangeness within
is different from the strangeness without. Without
it may be called a miracle ; within, it is a marvel.
That which had been new in and from the beginning
determined now to be new also in another manner
without losing the old. It was not to be only as a

Victim that he subjected himself to the choice of his
creatures. He accepted the terms of the creation
whom he had limited his omnipotence to create ; in
that sense he accepted justice. If he meant to sustain
his creatures in the pain to which they were reduced,
at least he also gave himself up to that pain. The
First Cause was responsible for them ; he accepted
responsibility and endured equality.

Creator and Victim then : the third function went
with those two. He would not only endure ; he
would renew ; that is, accepting their act he would
set up new relations with them on the basis of that act.
In their victimisation, and therefore in his, he proposed
to effect an escape from that victimisation. They had
refused the co-inherence of the original creation, and
had become (literally) incoherent in their suffering.
He proposed to make those sufferings themselves
co-inherent in him, and therefore to reintroduce them
into the principle which was he. The Incarnation
was to be a Redemption as well. He became flesh
for our sakes as well as his own. In this sense all
that has ever been said about his condescension was
true. He " condescended " to be involved intimately
in acts so repugnant to his nature that, could they have
been brought to a victorious ultimate conclusion, they
must have destroyed that nature. Prevented from
that by the stability of his divine nature, they would
inevitably destroy their authors. Prevented from
that by his sustaining power, they must eat into the
life that was he.

He was indeed the actual life ; or at least the life
that was his gift to that human superfluity came under
his government and resisted the Fall. Our whole

fundamental mode of existence was divine. Man,
rejecting him, rejected also the natural life. It is not
perhaps going too far to say that, in that too-fatal
hour, men and women were set against such simple
things as breathing, as their original body and blood.
Our physical nature was dragged down with our
spiritual and laboured, as it labours still, in a state it
was never meant to endure. The Incarnacy was to
redeem the flesh from what it had not invoked as well
as the soul from what it had. But at least our flesh
again and again supports the Redemption ; it bears
witness to glories ; it flashes now and then with the
heaven to which it is native ; and the great compact
of Virtues, the physical formula of beatitude, exiled
from its unity, yearns—and more innocently than the
soul—for its original joy.

Creator, Victim, and Redeemer then. But how
would the sin fare ? Sin is the name of a certain
relationship between man and God. When it is
fixed, if it is, into a final state, he gives it other names ;
he calls it *hell* and *damnation*. But if man were to be
restored, what was to happen to the sin ? He had a
name for that relationship too ; like a second Adam
indeed he named the beasts of our nature as they
wandered in the ruined Paradise ; he called this
" forgiveness." " Thy sins are forgiven thee ; go
in peace." One of the greatest poets has shown us
what he understood that word " forgiveness " to mean
in human terms. But what did the inventor of the
word, since he was the inventor of the thing, mean by
it ? Something at least by which the sin was to be
brought into perfect accord with the original good,
the incoherence into the co-inherence, the opening hell

into the opened heaven. Nothing else, obviously, would serve, for that, simply, was what had to be done. Continuing inflexibly upon the lines he had laid down for himself, he proceeded to do it.

IV.   THE OFFERING OF BLOOD

It is always possible to read the Gospels with our minds on one particular element in the unique person of the God–Man.   New meanings present themselves in relation to the whole when certain phrases are studied with respect to a part, to our Lord as Love, as Power, as Will.   It seems possible therefore to consider his life, or rather the records of it, in relation to him as Forgiveness.

It is, from our present point of view, not yet at all certain what the word means.   All that we take for granted is that the Trinity had determined the Incarnation of the Word, that They had determined and caused the creation of superfluous mankind with a purpose of entire joy, that mankind had set itself in such a relation to Them and especially to the flesh of the Word that it was bound, if the creation so ordained continued, to victimise its Creator, and that They had accepted that result and had determined that the original Incarnation should be a Redemption also ; that is, that his life on earth should redeem life and earth.   He was to be born, as he had willed, of a Mother.

The song in which the father of the Precursor, filled by Them with the divine Vision, praised the coming Thing asserted this.   The Precursor was to prophesy and prepare for the coming of the Lord as the coming of salvation " in the remission of their sins."   God's " heart of mercy " (as the marginalia

of the Revised Version calls it) was to be that in which
the day shone upon those " in darkness and in the
shadow of death." By the vision which appeared to
St. Joseph while he was meditating on the nature of
justice-in-love the same promise was given : " That
which is conceived in her is of the Holy Ghost . . .
she shall bring forth a son . . . it is he that shall save
his people from their sins." There was indeed something peculiarly applicable in the prophecy at that
moment. For St. Joseph " being a righteous man
and not willing to make her a public example, was
minded to put her away privily." If indeed the
princely saint—so young perhaps and perhaps so in
love—believing that he had been in some sense
" wronged " or at least deceived, desired no bitterness
and no open declaration of resentment, but a privy
hiding of a privy guilt, he had fulfilled much ; he had
set a great example to Christendom ; he had acted as
became all that was until that holy thing was born.

For before we come to the consideration of that
holy Thing, it is perhaps worth while to look a little
at what else had been. The present writer is incapable
of discussing the matter of pardon among savages and
aboriginal folk. There is, it seems, among many of
them penitence, confession, and reunion with the
society or with the god—and there are rites to that
effect. The question whether these are to be held
as imperfect representations of the Christian centre,
or whether Christianity is to be held merely as a more
intellectual, and even philosophical, development of
those rites, is a question which has been discussed
almost since Christianity appeared and seems likely
to be discussed as long as Christianity—or any

opposition to Christianity—remains. It depends so much on the *parti pris* that there is in fact little use in the discussion. It is one of the great advantages (or disadvantages) of Christianity that in the last resort it has no arguments ; it can do nothing but say, in the phrase which the Church claims that she only has the right and power to borrow from her Lord : " I am." If indeed the existence of God were certainly provable to human reason—but it cannot be ; at best, we cannot admit more than a reasonable likelihood. Faith is another kind of thing. Therefore the great disputes go on, and it is not impossible, though it rarely happens, that a man might accept by faith what his reason thought was unlikely. The split in our brain, as Siger of Brabant is said to have felt, is very deep. That does not do away with our duty to our brain.

That however is a digression. Anthropological discussion would be another digression. Whichever of the two above-mentioned alternatives is true, the main fact at present is the Christian decision. But before that was communicated—at least temporally— there existed the Jewish Law. This has been accepted by Christians, as a prelude to, and preparation for, the Christian ; not so, naturally, by the Jews to whom it belongs. But there are two points upon which something should be said, (i) the three elements of the Law—moral, natural, ritual—and the matter of sacrifice ; (ii) the prophetic idiom.

(i) The modern insistence on morals has caused to grow up a certain more or less defined suggestion that the moral element in the Law was of more value than the other. The Prophets, who particularly insisted

on it, are regarded as being in some sense more
advanced, even more " spiritual," than the priestly
schools with whom they are so often said to have
found themselves in opposition. But (speaking
without expert knowledge) there is in the original
Law, as it is presented to us in the Canonical writings,
no sign of this. " Impurity " may be moral or
ceremonial or natural. The real difference seems to
have been that for the serious moral offences there was
little chance of personal " atonement." The sentence
continually is death—death for idolatry, death for
witchcraft, death for incest, death for adultery, death
for murder. Other, and many, moral laws are laid
down, but there are few definite penalties attached to
them. It is, obscurely, the blood that is involved,
the blood that is important ; one might almost say
that wherever the blood is involved the Lord is
involved. Even the killing of a beast without
recognition of the Lord is made penal. " What man
soever there be of the house of Israel, that killeth an
ox, or lamb, or goat, in the camp, or that killeth it out
of the camp, and bringeth it not unto the door of the
tabernacle of the congregation, to offer an offering
unto the Lord before the tabernacle of the Lord ;
blood shall be imputed unto that man ; he hath shed
blood ; and that man shall be cut off from among his
people ; to the end that the children of Israel may
bring their sacrifices which they offer in the open
field, even that they may bring them unto the Lord,
unto the door of the tabernacle of the congregation,
unto the priest, and offer them for peace offerings
unto the Lord."

This certainly is a ceremonial more than a moral

uncleanness, and there seems to be some reason to suppose it was afterwards abrogated. The main point, however, is that, in most of the matters of uncleanness of any weight, blood was to be offered : the blood of the sinner or the blood of the sacrifice for the sinner, the blood in the place of judgement or the blood before the Mercy Seat. At the same time no member of that elect Society, " the congregation of the children of Israel," was to eat anything with blood in it ; " the blood thereof, which is the life thereof, ye shall not eat." " I will even set my face against that soul that eateth blood, and will cut him off from among his people. For the life of the flesh is in the blood : and I have given it to you upon the altar to make an atonement for your souls : for it is the blood that maketh an atonement for the soul. Therefore I said unto the children of Israel, No soul of you shall eat blood, neither shall any stranger that sojourneth among you eat blood."

Whoever ate the blood of an animal was to be cut off ; whoever shed the blood of a man was to be cut off. The blood belonged to the Lord throughout all animals and all men ; it was the life of the flesh and it made atonement for the soul. It was sprinkled before God for the soul, instead of the soul ; that is, as a substitution for the soul. The expiation for the sins of the soul (since sin was necessarily of the soul) was by the life of the flesh, either by the flesh that was in union with the soul that had sinned or by some other. Man must not kill man ; except by solémn decree as laid down in the Law or in war which was recognised by the Law. He might kill animals, but he must recognise their existence by recognising the

Creator of them ; it was a permission and not a right.

The high Day of Atonement carried this idea to the innermost places. It was then that the two goats were to be chosen, the one to be sacrificed for a sin-offering, the other to be driven into the wilderness carrying the sins of the people. It was then that the high-priest was to go in to where the cloud on the mercy seat was interpenetrated with the glory of the Lord, and sprinkle with his finger seven times " upon the mercy seat eastward " the blood of a bullock for himself and for his house, and afterwards the blood of the goat for the sins of the people " because of the uncleanness of the children of Israel, and because of their transgressions in all their sins ; and so shall he do for the tabernacle of the congregation, that remaineth among them in the midst of their uncleanness."

The sprinkling of blood seven times from the high priest's finger before the mercy seat where between the wings of the golden cherubim the Shekinah half-concealed and half-revealed itself in cloud reduced the blood-offering to its most ritual and least visible form. But it did not alter the essence ; that remained. The forgiveness of sins demanded it ; without shed-ding of blood is no remission of sins. The suspension of sacrifice since the fall of the Temple leaves the Law still supreme ; the decree is not altered in Israel. Nor elsewhere.

This ceremonial, because spiritual, importance of the blood, seems to apply generally. Almost any natural " shedding of blood " is regarded as " unclean." Even surgical blood-shedding, unless perhaps it were confined to the priests, ought apparently to come under the same formal condemnation; not perhaps improperly, for it is, as the need for it is, a result of the Fall. A bleeding from the nose would be unclean. Yet war was permitted, and executions? They were permitted by the particular will of the Lord; they were permitted by the Law which determined what was permissible. The children of Israel only slew " in the name of the Lord." There is also, of course, that other great natural bloodshed common to half the human race—menstruation. That was unclean. But it is not impossible that that is an image, naturally, of the great bloodshed on Calvary, and perhaps, supernaturally, in relation to it. Women share the victimisation of the blood; it is why, being the sacrifice so, they cannot be the priests. They are mothers and, in that special sense, victims; witnesses, in the body, to the suffering of the body, and the method of Redemption.

(ii) The idiom of the prophets is, as was said above, of another kind. There has everywhere tended to be a division, if not an actual conflict, between the prophets and the priests. It took place in Israel and outside Israel, and it has taken place in Christendom. What exactly the prophesyings in the early Church were we do not know. We do know that the organisation of Christendom proceeded on sacerdotal lines, frequently opposed or complemented by prophetic outbreaks. Neither mode of religion is, it seems, entirely adequate without the other; neither can remain at its best without the help of the other. There must be something all but automatic, as there must be something anything but automatic. It is,

of course, much easier to demand a prophet than a
priest; and it is far, far easier to become a pseudo-
prophet than a pseudo-priest. I will not say that
almost anyone can be a priest; it would not be true
for the priesthood is a vocation. But certainly almost
anyone can imagine himself to be a prophet.

It has not pleased God to build either the congregation of Israel or the fellowship of the Church on
prophets. They are the warning, the correction, the
voice in the wilderness. Occasionally they occur in
the ranks of the priesthood—Augustine is an example.
It is often true that they recall the attention of the
faithful to certain facts which are becoming blurred
or forgotten. They trouble the customary ritual
with a new sound. They are loved and hated at once,
and both by good men. They pronounce, generally,
the need of man to repent and be turned. It was this
which was the overpowering note in the prophets of
the Old Testament. Among the steady sacrifices
and the habitual assemblies they asked passionately
what, in fact, the pious worshippers were supposed to
be doing : in the very midst, as it were, of the Temple
courts, they cried out : " Turn ye, turn ye ; why will
ye die ? " In the very places where the convention
of centuries slew and entreated and shook blood from
its fingers, they declared that this also could be an
evil and a danger of death. " It is iniquity ; even the
solemn meeting."

The phrase is so familiar that we have perhaps lost
a sense of the terror. The Holy One, in the eyes of
the prophets, was rejecting the means of reconciliation
he had himself decreed ; the Shekinah over the Mercy
Seat shuddered back from the goats' blood that lay

before it. But not for the sake of the goat. It is not the shedding of blood that is wrong; only its indecent, its unbecoming, shedding. When the same Isaiah cries out in the name of the Holy One : " When ye make many prayers I will not hear; your hands are full of blood," it is repudiation of the blood of the sacrifice because of the blood on the hands that offer it. It is a too-easy interpretation that sees in the delighting-not in the blood " of bullocks or of lambs or of he-goats" a more spiritual mode of approach. The prophet demands only what the Rite had already demanded—a repentance, a turning back to the Lord : " Wash you; make you clean." The furniture of the Temple had included the laver; cleansed hands were to sprinkle the ancient blood. But since the Law and the Rites had been formulated they had been forgotten,—though the condition of the sacrifice was perennial and permanent. " Thou shalt bring Aaron and his sons," ran the Law, " unto the door of the tabernacle of the congregation, and wash them with water." " Wash you; make you clean," ran the new emphasis—but it was precisely a new emphasis on the old law. Bloody hands— hands stained with the blood of slain men, or guilty of blood thinned by slavery—were not fit to touch the sacrificial blood. It was precisely in the state of those fingers that the awful secret of obedience, of the accepted atonement, lay.

Yet there, though the hands were bloody with the life of men, lay still the single chance : " though your sins be as scarlet, they shall be as white as snow; though they be red like crimson, they shall be as wool." The congregation of Israel, the City of God,

had carried on the old original idolatry ; it had been
apostate. " How is the faithful city become an
harlot ! It was full of judgement ; righteousness
lodged in it ; but now murderers." It was to this
renewed state of evil, in which even reconciliation
had become iniquity, that the appeal of the High and
Holy One was addressed : " come now and let us
reason together." The Glory upon the Mercy-Seat
addressed itself to the double blasphemy before it ;
it exhibited the necessity of alteration, of obedience,
of the good ; it deigned to dispute with the sinner as
it had not with the righteous man Job. The distinction is not unjustified. It is in the nature of man, as
he knows himself, to demand an explanation, even a
justification, from the Lord. But the state in which
he can argue is not the state in which he repents ; the
conditions are different. No doubt the prophets of
Israel were reasonable as the apologists of Christianity
have been reasonable. But within the courts of
reason lay the laver and the veil of the Holy of Holies ;
there things had to be *done*. The ministers of the
Church should perhaps have been more sceptical and
intelligent than they have altogether been ; they
should have practised, more than they have, the
delicate incredulity which is the proper decency of the
mind. If proof of this were needed, their history
supplies it ; the terrible history of the witch-persecu-
tions, for example, when for lack of that incredulity
a delirium of vengeance filled the Church and her
ministers tortured the innocent as well as the guilty
(if to torture an innocent man is indeed worse than to
torture—to put to agonising and continuous pain—
a guilty man). But when this has been said, it remains

that this applies only to the outer courts ; the courtesies of love are not the kiss of the beloved. And the veil about the sanctuary is not the same as the things done within it.

There was expostulation for the sinner ; there were only taunts for Job ; the nearer to the centre the farther from an argument. Ezekiel himself did but renew the old bidding ; he is one of the tenderest and most human of the prophets ; he is full of lordly promises and of beauty, but the book called by his name ends with a description of " the frame of a city," and in the city a house and in the house an altar, and the glory over it, but the blood of a young bullock sprinkled there. " And the name of the city from that day shall be, The Lord is there."

This union of the turning of the sinner with the offering for sin meant then the forgiveness of the sin. But what, even so, is the forgiveness of the sin ? It is, in the prophets, generally its " putting-away," a " forgetting." " I am he that blotteth out thy transgressions . . . and will not remember thy sins " ; " I will remember their sins no more," the scarlet is to vanish, the crimson to die away. In the great healing and restoration which he has promised, the High and Holy One will set aside even the memory of the sin. This depends certainly on Israel's repentance ; but once that is in process, the past is to be remembered no more. " Behold, I create new heavens and a new earth : and the former shall not be remembered nor come into mind. But be ye glad and rejoice for ever in that which I create ; for behold I create in Jerusalem a rejoicing and her people a joy." The vision of a universal peace, and of the

holy community restored is everywhere : " a kingdom
of priests, a holy nation." The lordly passages in
which that future is described are too well known to
be quoted. They depend however on something like
a hypothetical restoration of innocence ; all the evil
is to be removed ; man, once he has repented, is to be
treated as if he had not sinned.

Certainly the phrases so used of oblivion may stand
for something else, for a seclusion into himself of the
Lord's knowledge of the sin. The iniquity is to be
covered in him. It must be admitted that in these
passages there is very little allusion to the sacrificial
" propitiation " ; and it is this perhaps which has
helped to give the prophets their reputation for
superior spirituality. The genius of Isaiah especially
carries the similes and metaphors of the restored peace
into an almost infinite sense of exalted natural goodness : " they shall not labour in vain nor bring forth
for trouble ; for they are the seed of the blessed of the
Lord, and their offspring with them. And it shall
come to pass, before they call I will answer, and while
they are yet speaking I will hear . . . they shall not
hurt nor destroy in all my holy mountain, saith the
Lord." This is the image of the consummation and
it is as good as any other image of that unthinkable
state. But the effect of the removal of any allusion
to the sacrifice is one of two things : either (i) the
Lord himself has forgotten the sin ; or (ii) only he
remembers it, and that only to himself ; his mercy
is to spare his people the recollection.[1]

[1] There are, of course, the "Suffering Servant" passages of Isaiah.
But I have spoken of them in relation to the same theme in another place
and do not wish to repeat the passage in this book. From our present
point of view it makes little difference whether those few passages darkly

Speaking therefore very generally, we may say that in the Old Testament the Forgiveness is regarded in one of two ways. The sin (by definition) having been committed, the schism between God and men having (by definition) been opened, there remain judgement and mercy. The judgement is to leave the sinner to the sin, to the ruin and the exile and the pain. The Mercy operates in one of two ways, which are not exclusive and not, in the Old Testament, regarded as being exclusive, but are differently stressed in different parts. The first is the Rite of blood. It is not, so far as can be seen, very clearly explained, nor indeed could be. But the blood which is the life is to be offered as an atonement for the soul; and the blood of bullocks and goats is to be offered as a vicarious sacrifice instead of the blood of men. The whole burden of this approach is that without shedding of blood is no remission of sins.

The other way stresses something else. The very sacrifice of Reconciliation itself has, because of man's sin, become iniquity. " He that killeth an ox is as if he slew a man; he that sacrificeth a lamb as if he cut off a dog's neck; he that offereth an oblation as if he offered swine's blood; he that burneth incense as if he blessed an idol. Yea, they have chosen their own ways, and their soul delighteth in their abominations." The whole point of that passage is that the very substance of the sacrifice has been changed from clean to unclean. It is not consideration for the animals or disapproval of the blood that speaks; or what could be said about the dog or the pig? It is

foretold the Redeemer or not. The general tone of the prophet is, I think, as has been stated.

the Rite which has been turned into uncleanness. " I also will choose their delusions "—one of the more appalling phrases of the Bible.

Or, even if the actual Rite has not been transformed, yet men use it without regard for the spiritual conversion that should accompany it. God cannot, or at least will not, put away man's sin unless man has put it away, or at least attempted to put it away. Social and individual iniquities make the Rite and the Pardon a delusion. " I will choose their delusions " ; I will agree that the Forgiveness shall be a delusion, that they shall think it has been and it shall not have been. From that still worse evil repentance nevertheless may yet save. Then the operating sacrifices shall continue ; the blood of animals or (in those Servant passages of Isaiah) the blood of something other than animals is effective to the cleansing ; and the knowledge is covered. It is covered from God's people, and it is covered either from God himself or in God himself. This is the offered covenant.

The blood on the altar and the seclusion of the sin to God—these then are the two points of the Old Testament : all that had been up to St. Joseph and the Birth. St. Joseph had precisely intended the seclusion. But that which now appeared on the earth was the original both of blood and seclusion. The Birth which now took place was of the body which was the Incarnation that had been intended from the beginning ; and its blood was in its nature. The knowledge of the sins of men was that which, also from the beginning, had determined that the Incarnation should be a Redemption also. The Birth then into the outer world was a union of blood and knowledge. The priests and prophets had ordered the Rites and exhorted souls. But neither priest nor prophet knew what sin was ; only God knew that, for only God knew what had happened when man preferred something alien to the nature both of the Godhead and the Manhood of the Incarnation. They had chosen delusions and he had consented, at the cost of his blood and his knowledge enduring the Delusion, He condescended therefore to be what had been intended, to be the child of a mother.

It has been the habit of Christendom to regard that mother with peculiar veneration ; so much so that the Roman Church has declared, as a part of the Faith, that she was conceived immaculately, that is, without vestige of original sin, and very many non-Roman Christians either accept the same belief or would find no great difficulty in accepting it. It may, humbly, be supposed that so high, so original, a miracle had about it some such particular purpose as that his human affections should have no barrier to their direct operation. He who wished to exercise all human virtues would not be without the virtue of *pietas ;* his Manhood venerated what his Godhead had sustained and saved, achieving (it is said) in the instant of her conception what he achieves, sooner or later, in all redeemed souls. There was in the Roman Church in the 17th century a particular devotion to the Heart of Jesus and Mary : the single word united the double devotion of love. There was, I suppose, between them nothing for either to forgive ; yet on that unforgiving love all other loves depended. It is the only case in which the word can be used except with a sense of hardness ; there it is even more tender

than its opposite. Certainly that also has its meaning ;
it reminds us still of humility. Love that forgives,
which is the only love we can, or can ever, know, is
tender and beautiful ; but Love that has nothing to
forgive can be—I will not say, unconfined in any part,
for confined love is not love but—less characterised
by the recollection of its opposite. The mystery of
such a love is as unimaginable as our pre-fallen state ;
and the climax of matter depended on it. There
sprang from it the very flash of Forgiveness. She
who in the free exercise of her choice loved her
Creator because he chose that she should, became
the mother of his Incarnation, the mother therefore
of his victimisation and redemption.

He became then Forgiveness in flesh ; he lived the
life of Forgiveness. This undoubted fact serves as
a reminder that Forgiveness is an act, and not a set
of words. It is a thing to be *done*. It may be done
easily or with difficulty, but there is only one alternative to its being done, and that is its *not* being done.
It is as much a thing happening as a birth is. " The
spirit of forgiveness " is, no doubt, a beautiful thing,
but it does not exist except in acts—at any rate, as far
as we are concerned. The acts, in fact, especially
when done with a certain sense of self-compulsion,
are all we know of the spirit. The birth of Forgiveness was the birth of something of flesh and blood,
of brain and bone. It appeared in the world at a
certain time and place—in the world which we know
as time and place. And it proceeded to live a life
characterised (we are to believe) by acts and words
which, in their relation to men throughout, were
precisely Forgiveness. It exactly claimed this power,

and it called it a power, an energy: "that ye may know that the Son of Man hath power on earth to forgive sins"; "thy sins be forgiven thee." This ascription to himself is like the similar ascription to himself of powers not certainly to break the law, but certainly of some right to control it. He says, for instance, that the Son of Man is lord of the Sabbath, but that the Sabbath was made for man, and not man for the Sabbath. He identifies himself with man, but he never equalises man with himself, and this is true of forgiveness also. He commands men to forgive debts owed to them, but in the parable as in the Lord's Prayer, that forgiveness depends on their own debts being forgiven. He declares it to be a source, but man is to use it as a measure. This indeed is the secret of all the difference: he does not measure himself by man but man by himself. He certainly is the identity but it is for man to discover him so. "With what measure ye mete, it shall be measured to you again; good measure, pressed down and running over, shall men give into your bosom." We can choose another measure than himself at our own risk. It is the assent of the Divine Son to the kind of measurement demanded by the rebel angels which Milton used to precede their overthrow.

> Therefore to me their doom he hath assigned,
> That they may have their wish, to try with me
> In battle which the stronger proves, they all
> Or I alone against them, since by strength
> They measure all, of other excellence
> Not emulous, nor care who them excels;
> Nor other strife with them do I vouchsafe.

V. FORGIVENESS IN MAN

THERE is no space here to study all the records of
that Life in terms of Forgiveness, nor indeed could
anything of the sort be properly done except after
years of attention; the danger of the invention of
neat morals and pretty metaphysics is too great. But
certain incidents in that Life stand out. It was the
Life that was the fact—of Forgiveness as of everything holy else, and there was no moment in that Life
which was not, towards men and women, a fact of
Forgiveness, or at least a fact of the offer of Forgiveness. It proceeded steadily towards the consummate
Forgiveness and the consummate Reconciliation, but
they were not apart from the Life.

The Temptation, for example, is precisely, among
other things, a temptation of Forgiveness, an effort
to turn Forgiveness into something other than itself.
All temptations are, in a sense, the same; they all
depend on the rousing of some false hope, and on
some action for its satisfaction. The order of the
three temptations in the Canonical Writings cannot
be of first importance, or we should not have been
given two different accounts; we may presumably
use each for edification without denying the other.
The first temptation of Forgiveness then is to procure,
through its own operation, some immediate comfort.
The stones—let us say, the stones of offence—which
are in the way are to be turned at once into bread.
They are to perform the office of bread and not of

stones. No doubt something like this may eventually happen to the holy soul; no doubt, in the end, the very stones themselves become nourishing. The nourishment derived at last from that hard strong state which can be described as " stones " may be found to be much superior to that easier appeasement of natural hunger described as " bread." Our natural hunger desires immediate comfort. Yet any haste after this comfort is apt to destroy the whole act of forgiveness. It may often be easier for us to forgive than not—easier because more comfortable; nor is it always wrong to do so, any more than it is wrong to eat bread. But to pretend to forgive for the sake of one's own comfort is nonsense. " Man does not live by bread alone but by every word that proceedeth out of the mouth of God "; that is, by God's knowledge of sin and forgiveness. It may be possible to return to that point presently.

The Second Temptation, let us say, is the setting on the pinnacle of the Temple; this is the order in St. Matthew. The principle of this is that the Son of God should " tempt " God; that Forgiveness should presume on its own nature instead of referring all to God's will. It assumes that it will be sustained by the divine messengers; nay, it assumes that the divine messengers will be there to support *it*. Inconceivable as it may seem that the humanity of the Son of God should feel that temptation, yet we must believe that he did, or the whole thing is false. But for us this temptation is probably even more common than the first; the worse temptations are always the commonest. The first was a kind of Sloth; this is Pride. Pride is the besetting sin of Pardon, almost

the infernal twin of Pardon ; it is its consciousness ;
rather, say, its self-consciousness become its only
consciousness. It is the condescension, the *de haut
en bas* element, which is with so much difficulty
refused. After all, if one has been injured, if one has
suffered wrong ? " Cast thyself down," the devil
murmurs, " the angels will support you ; be noble
and forgive. You will have done the Right Thing ;
you will have behaved better than the enemy." So,
perhaps ; but it will not be the angels of heaven who
will support that kind of consciousness, unless by a
fresh reference of ourselves to Forgiveness. " Thou
shalt not tempt the Lord thy God."

The Third Temptation is not perhaps so common.
The false hope of comfort, the false hope of
superiority ; and now ? The false hope of freedom,
but a freedom given by the devil. Can Forgiveness
worship the devil ? all the virtues can worship the
devil. Was not the Incarnate tempted ? and is one
to suppose the temptation was not real ? No ; in
some sense Forgiveness is promised the kingdoms of
this world ; and how ? Precisely by being set free
from grudges and resentments, from bitterness and
strife. This certainly is the proper nature and the
proper result of Forgiveness, but than also Forgiveness which *primarily* desired that would not be forgiveness at all. It is but the mere point of *whom* one
adores, the very last point, so small, yet so much all.
It is the " having nothing yet possessing all things " of
St. Paul turned into a maxim of personal greed. If
one could achieve that state one would be completely
free, one would no longer be hurt by others. To be,
or to desire to be, free from being hurt by others, is

to be, or to desire to be, free from the co-inherence of all human souls, which it was the express intention of Christ to redeem. In the perfect redemption, no doubt we all shall be free so ; and when all, then each one. But till all, none. The achievement would be exactly hell; it would be to desire something other than he. "Thou shalt worship the Lord thy God and him only shalt thou serve."

Such then were the temptations he rejected, the delusions he would not choose. He exhibited delusion as delusion ; he left the Church to declare what delusion was. It has not done it, or it has ; the discussions on its fidelity or apostasy need not detain us here. He himself exhibited the facts of existence. Neither comfort nor pride nor detachment were to interfere with them ; if they did, the facts would combine with the delusions to bring about hell. Yet he restored what was permissible ; the first of the marvellous works did but increase enjoyment. He did not merely give men wine ; when they had already drunk wine, he gave them more and better wine. He who would not make bread for himself would make wine for others. "Others he saved ; himself he could not save."

All this matter of the Temptation was, in our sacred Lord, after its own and central kind, and indeed must still remain so. No definition or dogma can explain to us how Forgiveness was tempted not to be Forgiveness, and Love not to be Love. We only know that he maintained his exact function ; he remained free. He remained free, that is, to proclaim forgiveness—free to derive that power from his Father, free to exercise it towards us. When he had returned to

his public life he began to do so : notably, in the case
of the man sick of the palsy. It was one of those
occasions on which he definitely declared that the
miracle was a sign of something else. It will be
remembered that the sick man had been lowered
through the roof by his bearers ; and the narrative
proceeds : " And when he saw their faith [not, for
whatever the distinction is worth, his alone, if his at
all], he said unto him, Man, thy sins are forgiven thee.
And the scribes and Pharisees began to reason, saying,
Who is this which speaketh blasphemies ? Who can
forgive sins, but God alone ? But when Jesus per-
ceived their thoughts, he answering said unto them,
What reason ye in your hearts ? Whether is easier
to say, Thy sins be forgiven thee ; or to say, Rise up
and walk ? But that ye may know that the Son of
man hath power upon earth to forgive sins (he said
unto the sick of the palsy), I say unto thee, Arise,
and take up thy couch, and go unto thy house. And
immediately he rose up before them, and took up
that whereon he lay, and departed to his own house,
glorifying God. And they were all amazed, and they
glorified God, and were filled with fear, saying, We
have seen strange things to-day."

The " strange things " were the double renovation
of power—the sign that the sins are forgiven is the
healing of the palsy. The proclamation is of a fact,
a fact coming after another fact, that of faith ; and
out of this strangeness spring amazement and glorifying and holy awe. The record reads not altogether
unlike certain moments of experience in our own lives
—directly religious or indirectly religious ; the
moment of the vision, one way or another, of power.

It is a matter for some consideration whether we do not often fail to grasp that power, whether we lose (if we do) the effect of renovation, precisely because we do not afterwards root our experience in the forgiveness of our sins. The Glory appears, but we can only belong to it by virtue of being united to it as a whole ; that is, by the evil as by the good ; by sins as by virtues. It is the movement of sin towards it which is called repentance ; it is the movement of the good towards it which is called faith. The consciousness of repentance—that is, the consciousness of sin in love ; that is, of the forgiveness of sin—is the preservation of humility ; it is the glass in which we can see darkly something of that great virtue which we can never see in itself.

The " strange things " were the reunion of the sick of the palsy, physically and spiritually, with the Glory of God. It was a renovation of spirit and flesh, and all the rest of the Gospels is like it, for all the rest is the account of the Glory so united or of the means of the uniting or of the rejection of the uniting. It comes as a renewal of nature as well as of supernature ; it changes water into wine for those who have already drunk wine, and multiplies food for those who are in need of food. It comes " eating and drinking " ; it is even denounced as " a gluttonous man and a wine-bibber." It is no longer, as it had been under the Jewish Law, a hidden thing ; the proclamation of the kingdom was that everything should be known. All—" every secret thing "—is to be brought out into clarity. It is in this clarity and charity, between men as between God and men, that " the high dignity and never-ceasing perpetuity of our nature " consists.

One thing alone he hid, as it were, from his exhibition
of himself in his kingdom, the mysterious sin against
the Holy Ghost. As there had been a possibility of
disobedience in the original creation, as there had been
a possibility of iniquity in the Rites of the Jewish Law,
so there was a possibility of final rejection in this
restored creation. There was still an obscene outrage
which man might insist on finding and choosing ; he
hinted and hid it.

And what then was the forgiveness of which this
was the power ? It has been greatly described by
William Law.[1]

" What is God's forgiving sinful man ? It is nothing
else in its whole nature but God's making him
righteous again. There is no other forgiveness of
sin but being made free from it. Therefore, the
compassionate love of God that forgives sin is no
other than God's love of his own righteousness, for
the sake of which and through the love of which
he makes man righteous again. This is the one
righteousness of God that is rigorous, that makes
no abatements, that must be satisfied, must be fulfilled
in every creature that is to have communion with
him. And this righteousness that is thus rigorous is
nothing else but the unalterable purity and perfection
of the divine love which, from eternity to eternity,
can love nothing but its own righteousness, can will
nothing but its own goodness, and therefore can will
nothing towards fallen man but the return of his lost
goodness by a new birth of the divine life in him,
which is the true forgiveness of sins. For what is
the sinful state of man ? It is nothing else but the

[1] *Selected Writings of William Law Letter IV.* Stephen Hobhouse.

loss of that divine nature which cannot commit sin ;
therefore, the forgiving man's sin is, in the truth and
reality of it, nothing else but the revival of that nature
in man which, being born of God, sinneth not."

This is what he lived ; what was the conclusion of
the life ? It is very well known ; it is the crucifixion
of the power to forgive. Certainly, the enemies of
Christ did not realise it as that ; it was indeed their
reason for rejecting him, or one of their reasons for
rejecting, that he claimed that power and proclamation.
They declared that none could forgive sins but God
alone. He also declared the same thing ; he referred
that, as he referred all, to his Father. The agreement
on principle was complete ; all controversy was on
the question of the authority of Christ to declare what
he also declared he did not, so far, originate. He
declared himself to be its voice, its operation ; they
asserted that he was its contradiction, and a blasphemy.
The dispute remains. Either he was indeed that
Forgiveness in action or he improperly arrogated to
himself that deific annunciation. It may be observed
that it was a thing he never asked from men—he who
was continually proclaiming his own humility. He
taught men to forgive each other ; he made it a
necessity of the kingdom ; he withdrew hope from
those who would not understand that necessity. But
he never suggested that he himself should be forgiven
—by any man or any god ; he assumed, lucidly and
wholly, that there was nothing to forgive and none
who could forgive. Nor did he ever quite forgive.
He never did say : " I forgive you." He who talked
of himself continually never spoke of himself in that.
He said : " Father, forgive . . ." All the sin was

elsewhere; all the penitence must be elsewhere;
all the pardon was elsewhere. God forgave; he
declared forgiveness; men were to be forgiven.

He concentrated upon himself the two ideas which
had marked the Jewish tradition. Sins had been
forgiven by virtue of the blood; " it is the blood
that maketh atonement for the soul." The result of
that atonement had been the seclusion of the knowledge of the sin into God. The angelic glories of
heaven had proclaimed before the birth of Jesus that
he had come to save his people from their sins; he
himself declared that he had come to die : " the Son
of Man *must* . . ." His agelong victimisation was
perfected. It had been of old a cause for denunciation
of the faithful by the prophets that they had defiled
with non-sacrificial blood the altar of the sacrificial;
that the solemn meeting had been made iniquity and
that the Rites had become obscene. The new Rite
was indeed hidden. None upon earth (unless indeed
the Divine Mother—but there is nothing to show it,
and something against it)—none upon earth knew
that the awful and unique Rite was in process of
presentation. It was secluded within his own knowledge alone. But it was a closer union than any the
ancient Law had known or decreed. For this was
not only the blood of the sacrifice making atonement
for the original sin ; it was the insulted sacrifice still
making atonement for itself. Doubly misused, it
was doubly powerful. Its power was in itself; the
sacrifice sacrificed itself. " It was in his power," said
Augustine, " to be affected in this or that way or not."
In the old Rites the blood of the offering and the
consequent forgiveness had been separate things;

their connection had been, or rather had seemed, almost arbitrary. It may be, because of it, that the whole animal creation has indeed a greater place than we know; the feast of the Holy Innocents ought perhaps to be thought to include those calves and goats and bulls who died, unknowingly, too soon, and, unknowingly, for vicarious satisfaction. They were symbolical? alas, they were living! they were of less value? we owe them still their own; they were sacrificed by command of the Will? it may be that the Will recollects them, and it was not perhaps without reason that it was forbidden to the faithful of the Old Dispensation to eat the blood; it was not safe until their Maker had also given us his. If that great Feast of the children who also did not will to die, and did not know for whom they died, and yet have been canonised because of that ignorant death— if that feast cannot be extended to include the sacrificed beasts, then it might not be altogether a useless act of devotion to God if the Church recollected before him one day in the year the irrational innocents who also died. He certainly whose sacred blood was not without relationship to theirs may have recollected them when he concluded their blood with his own, when the veil of the temple, behind which the mystery was wrought, was at last rent; and all was exposed—sin and repentance and sacrifice and pardon.

He substituted then his knowledge for their ignorance; his full consciousness for their partial; his reason for their unreason. The Forgiveness became the sacrifice. It is worth while to consider that precisely the Forgiveness was then—must one say *endangered?* How else—if at all his temptation

and his trial were real ? In some sense, that must be
true which can only be expressed by saying that the
possibility of his Redemption *might* have been an
impossibility. He *might* have chosen, at any moment,
not to continue ; he *might* have prayed for the twelve
legions of angels ; he *might*, in fact, have descended
from the cross, before he was deposed thence. But
these things are for the theologians ; it is sufficient
here to note only (however it be phrased) that possible
impossibility. Or, if we must not say even so much,
yet at least it is worth while to contemplate for a
moment the entire disappearance and negation of
Forgiveness. That, after all, was what his slayers
were, unknowingly, about. For the best of motives
or the worst, or in some confusion between (but, for
reasons given elsewhere, I would rather think the
best), they were engaged in the entire destruction of
Forgiveness. The atonement of the Temple was
being contradicted by their purpose in this new Rite
as it was being fulfilled by his purpose in the Rite.
Forgiveness between God and man, and forgiveness
therefore between man and man, would, had they
had their way, have ceased upon earth.

Contemplate for a moment the result. We under-
rate the things which, under the Mercy, are still
natural to us ; much more, in all the religions, supernatural ; much more, in the Christian Church, final.
Man remembers his ancient co-inherence still ; it is
not to say he need, nor that he often enough does.
But reconciliation is still recollected and present even
in a pagan world, in our own culture or in others.
The removal of reconciliation would have left us,
quite simply, unreconciled, and that everywhere and

not alone in religion. The present state of international anguish would have been universal, and that not only among nations. Every grudge and every resentment would have lasted ; the dream of anything else would have been but a dream, and a less recurrent dream. The possibility of love would have depended upon the lack of offence ; and no mortal lover but knows how easy offence is. The least rudeness would have rankled, and the very idea of anything else would have disappeared. We should have come to depend upon resentment ; therefore, upon hate ; therefore, on vengeance. This, which spreads fast enough even now, would then have spread with less and less difficulty and less and less delay. War, in the house and in the field, secret or open, malicious and continual, would have been our doom ; there would, simply, have been no alternative. We could never have forgiven our children nor our children us ; they would have been born into a world of malice, and their malice, had they survived, would have been directed against us. It is true they probably would not have survived ; their parents would have loathed them too soon and too well ; and, indeed, remove but that habit of reconciliation, and the begetting of children would soon have ceased. Sterile and stupid, the generations of men would have hastened into hell.

Such was the shadow of the great darkness over the cross, which lingers a little when the darkness is over and the Death alone is present. The suspension of his life allows us a space to consider it, but the nightmare ends with his Return. But his Return was from something other than nightmare. " His agony " wrote Law again, " was His entrance into the last eternal terrors of the lost soul, into the real horrors of that dreadful eternal death which man unredeemed must have died into when he left this world. We are therefore not to consider our Lord's death upon the Cross as only the death of that mortal body which was nailed to it, but we are to look upon Him with wounded hearts, as fixed and fastened in the state of that twofold death, which was due to the fallen nature, out of which He could not come till He could say ' It is finished ; Father, into thy hands I commend my spirit.' "

It was in this state that he forgave : forgave ? say, he loved and renewed those who had brought him into it ; he loved them so as to maintain them while they brought him into it, as he had maintained the tree that made the wood and the metal that made the nails. He forgave from the state of " the eternal terrors of the lost soul." He so forgave that he exchanged his love for man's loss ; he received the loss and gave the love. It is the mere nature of forgiveness ; there can be no other ; but then it was there, and therefore everywhere ; it is its nature— yes, but then its nature does so exist. No less, in our degree, will serve as our duty ; no less—unbearable glory !—is the true nature of our very life. But whatever distress his glory lays upon us in our present state, it cannot be anything like his state then nor as bad as our only alternative state. On the other hand, when he returned, he returned with his scars. The Resurrection is something other than the spiritual survival. It is the continuation of the physical in the highest degree ; the continuation of the past into the present. But the past was now exposed. His glory secluded the scars no more; therefore it did not seclude the sin that led to them. The blood had been shed; it had made atonement; but it was no longer to be lost, unnoticeably, like that of bulls and goats had been. It was, as the great scene with St. Thomas Didymus shows, and as the legend of St. Martin of Tours maintains, to be recollected for ever in the stigmata whence it had flowed. He revealed himself, at that time, obscurely, only to those who already knew him; the rest of mankind had yet to learn to know. It is his method always.

The Resurrection was the Resurrection of Forgiveness, but the sin which brought it about was no longer to be covered, even by and in God himself. He became an energy of forgiveness in the Church. He had stated the principle in the years of his life—almost, as it were, by accident, as an answer to a question or a clause in a prayer. That principle was that the active and passive modes of forgiveness were not to be separated; that they were indeed, in some sense, identical; one could not exist without the other. This was not a matter of language; it was a fact, a law of nature—anyhow, of redeemed nature. To forgive and to be forgiven were one thing. "And forgive us our sins as we forgive them that trespass against us." This was the entreaty and this was the answer to the entreaty. The comment on it had been in the parable of the Wicked Servant. The parable is not perhaps altogether consistent with our feelings; it may shock us that a man who has had his debts forgiven should have them again set against him. But the moral and metaphysical doctrine is exact; this is what happens. It is that state of things in action which the Lord's Prayer entreats to come into action. The threat implicit in that prayer—in that single clause—is very high; it is the only clause which carries a threat, but there it is clear. No word in English carries a greater possibility of terror than the little word " as " in that clause; it is the measuring rod of the heavenly City, and the knot of the new union. But also it is the key of hell and the knife that cuts the knot of union.

The condition of forgiving then is to be forgiven; the condition of being forgiven is to forgive. The two conditions are co-existent; they are indeed the very point of co-existence, the root of the new union, the beginning of the recovery of the co-inherence in which all creation had begun. Out of that point of double submission the City of God was to rise. Double submission? Yes, for in this the active was to be as submissive as the passive. The disciple had to be forgiven; he had also to forgive—both in obedience to the command of this Figure which was itself Forgiveness. The Figure was, and pronounced, a state of things; it was the new situation of man. That which Immanuel alone was, he alone could not passively experience. He expressed the prerogative of pardon; he could not submit to its necessity. Both prerogative and necessity were to be promulgated through the disciple. Our Lord conceded the new prerogative to the free-will already conceded at the creation. There had, then, been no need for it; there was, now, every need for it. Men could forgive each other by the same free will which, since the Fall, had been used for injuring each other. But the concession was also a command, as all the Divine concessions are ; it is not in the nature of God to concede possibilities of the first order which may be left unused. "Everyone which is perfect shall be as his Master," and perfection being the only thing he required, the disciple was to forgive, of his own choice, as well as, of his own choice, to be forgiven. The single Will acted in him in a double mode—and the disciple had only to obey. One might be agreeable and the other not, or they might both be agreeable, or neither ; that was of no importance. As in the Morning Joy and the Evening Joy, the individual, and, indeed, the whole world, opened out into the forgiveness asked from it, and turned to close again in the forgiveness granted to it—and these two were one.

Such was the single fundamental of the Church. The Church was the new world ; into the Church the whole old world was to be drawn. Anyone who was not rooted in that fundamental simply did not belong to the Church at all ; except again by new faith in that power of promulgation and by new repentance for having failed from that power. At first indeed the Church even doubted this. It was not, for some time, at all clear that there could be repentance and pardon after baptism. But it became tender in the end, as the great dialogue between Christ and Peter had taught it to be. Yet its tenderness was compulsive ; if there was to be no end to the operation on the divine side, nor was there to be on the human. "Seven times ? . . . seventy times seven"—in a day, in an hour, in a moment. As in old days the iniquity of the solemn meeting was itself a subject for repentance, so now was any failure of forgiveness.

The disciple might not achieve perfection, but he must mean perfection, so only would Immanuel achieve perfection in him. Without that he was not even a disciple; he was, by necessity, self-outcast. But with that he was able " to provoke unto love and good works," and to be provoked. The second is perhaps even more difficult than the first; the consciousness of having been forgiven is almost the only condition in which one can endure that provocation.

This then was the temper, the *ethos*, of the Church. The opposite temper, the alternative *ethos*, was expressed in the dulcet words : " With what measure ye mete, it shall be measured to you again; good measure, pressed down and running over. . . ." The sentence certainly covers both : measurement there certainly must be. Love is measurement in detail, as all good things are. Love is the smallest, and yet the most important, detail in the whole measurement of the universe. The exactitude of the measurement was the same anyhow; " no idle word " was to escape it. Everything was to be known; God had secluded in himself so long as he himself remained secluded. But now he had been exposed and exhibited—by his will, in flesh and birth; by man's will, in the death of flesh. The exposition of himself meant the exposition of all that was in himself —including the sin and the sacrifice he had deigned to become.

VI THE TECHNIQUE OF PARDON

YET, it may be said, forgiveness itself had to be measured, that is, to be understood; and it may be suggested in answer that there are three chief modes in which we do understand it in its own high and lofty style. The virtues, owing to the laborious detail in which they have to be pursued by us (and we can only pursue them in laborious detail—"general good," said Blake, "is the plea of the scoundrel, hypocrite, and flatterer")—the virtues are apt to be subdued to our own niggling style. But in themselves they are not so; they are gay and princely; and so they are seen when they are recognised in others simply because we are in a state of love towards others. We can admire them in their freedom in others when in ourselves they must seem, if not in servitude, at least only just escaped from servitude, sore from the manacles, bleeding from their effort at freedom, lame, purblind, unheavenly. It is our business to admire them heavenly whenever they can be so seen; the opportunity is in such states as marriage and friendship, and we do very well to take it whenever it is found. "This ought ye to have done, and not to have left the other undone." We must not cease from our own labour because the glory is seen free in another; but neither must we cease to admire the glory because the labour is all that we can feel in ourselves. Nevertheless we might uncon-

sciously learn to carry even grace with an air; it is
not ours, and so we may; we have nothing to be
proud of; another has laboured and we are entered
into his labour. An unconscious magnificence of any
virtue is only to be attained by the practice of that
virtue combined with humility. Since this is bound
to be conscious, it is not always easy to achieve its
opposite; but in itself the grace of " the weight of
glory " is precisely its lightness.

It may be suggested therefore that forgiveness can
be considered as applicable in three ways: (i) to
things which need not be forgiven; (ii) to things
which can be forgiven; (iii) to things which cannot
be forgiven. The first and the third, put so, are
contradictory; nevertheless, the phrases may for the
present stand.

(i) Things which need not be forgiven. There is
a tendency among some Christians to make a burden
of things which non-Christians would pass over
lightly. They overdo forgiveness as they overdo
patience and other virtues. No doubt Christianity
and life ought to be one; no doubt, essentially, they
are one; that is why we are at odds with both,
because we are still often at odds with that which is
the root of both. No doubt we ought to be always
looking for opportunities of leading the Christian life.
But there are two ways of doing even that—one is
with courtesy and the other without courtesy.
Courtesy is our whole business towards our neigh-
bours; it is indeed spiritual self-preservation; well,
but then so is love. Love, we have been told, is slow
to anger; it is, as a result, slow to forgive, for it will
not be in a hurry to assume that there is anything to

forgive ; and if there is, it will not be in a hurry to make a business of forgiving. Many lives are passed without the experience of anything in others which can seriously be supposed to need forgiveness, though not indeed without themselves committing wrongs which may seem to need forgiveness. I do not mean here only that we should not make an exterior fuss ; we should not even make an interior fuss. The good manners of the City of God are supernaturally instinctive ; the instinct of the new life should warn us of any approaching danger of pomposity or guile, and the danger is subtle. The new way—forgiveness, humility, clarity, charity—is there ; it is the old man on the new way who is the tempter, and who beguiles us away from it while we think we are walking on it. We cannot, and need not, when we seem to be insulted or injured, be unaware of it ; but we can dismiss the awareness with a shrug or a smile—at ourselves. "A sense of humour" has been overpraised ; wit would be better, could we attain it, but it must be a whole and healthy wit, and it should be but an instrument at first. Love "doth not behave itself unseemly" ; that is, it carries itself beautifully ; it takes no heed to itself. An awareness of injury, unless it has been deeply aimed at the heart, is exactly taking heed to oneself ; an awareness of forgiveness, unless it is asked, is apt to be a taking heed to itself. Not to be quick to forgive in this sense is as much a part of the divine command as not to be slow is in another ; we have to be free ; even from the virtues, in the end.

(ii) Things which can be forgiven. But how then to distinguish, to carry ourselves handsomely, to

avoid rejoicing in iniquity? Rejoicing in other
people's iniquity, one way or another, is a not uncom-
mon fault.   There is at least one simple distinction,
even if it cannot always be used; it lies in the request
for forgiveness.   St. Peter, in the dialogue with
Immanuel mentioned earlier, included this as a condition, and our Lord permitted it : " if my brother
sin against me and turn again ? " The question here
is of serious, but not fatal, harm; injuries which
wound but do not kill the heart; blows which might
be returned in anger but not with a cold and determined vengeance; such wounds as leave love, where
it is felt, still felt as in being.   We may be permitted
perhaps to take the term " my brother " as significant
there; at least, for the present purpose.   Say, that
the consciousness of brotherhood, of relationship, is
still vital; it is within that relationship that the harm
has been done.   It is then within that relationship
that the forgiveness must exist, and since all relationship must thrive or decay by what it holds within it,
by its elements, it is from such forgiveness that the
relationship must thrive.   But then, since mutual
love thrives from mutual acts, the forgiveness must
be a mutual act, an act of agreement.   Love, indeed,
in that sense, is mutuality; the effort to practise love
is an effort to become mutual; that is where it goes
beyond what is generally called " unselfishness."
To prefer another's will to one's own is much, but
to become another's will by means of one's own is
more, and is indeed the necessary thing for love.
" Love," said St. Thomas, " is nothing else than the
willing of good " to the beloved; and when the
functions of the beloved are exercised in the good,

there one must love the beloved in his or her functions ; one must will those functions, and be a power towards them. The union of lovers is in that double energy. It is true indeed that he is unwise who falls into the pseudo-romantic illusion of saying : " O I can only do it *if* . . ." ; who demands companionship before he can be industrious and love before he can be chaste. " They only can do it with you who can do it without you." But, that being so, there can be an added power ; as it were, the oxygen to the mountain-climber. No doubt, if one cylinder were not there, another would serve ; there is nothing sacrosanct about oneself ; anything might do as well. But if one is required to be oxygen, one had better be oxygen.

This where and as it applies. In some things it does not apply. Thus the most intense physical form of mutuality is, normally, in intercourse between the sexes ; the most perfected, there, that which results in childbirth. But the physical form is but one, and not, for all the mystery of the body, in the end the most important. Many separated lovers have discovered that. Of the spiritual functions, the realisation of a sense of sin is one, and of repentance, and of pardon. A double energy should go to it. This is not to say that it is the lover's business to impose a sense of sin on, or to demand it from, the beloved ; he would be a fool who was thus rash ; more especially he would be a fool who did so without a great and piercing sense of exchange. Guilt is in all ; it is the guilty who forgives. Entreated to forgive, by another as guilty, it is his whole duty to restore reconciliation by any and every means, for

ever and ever, without condition. The protested
single guilt on the part of another leads more easily
to a sense of one's own single guilt; therefore to a
sharing of the condition of guilt. The entreaty for
forgiveness does not, among mortal creatures, abolish
the sin, but it does a little transform it. It transforms
it doubly; it provokes a shy humility on the part not
only of the pardoned but of the pardoner. The
awful consciousness (in any serious matter) that he is
necessarily exercising, in his proper degree, the
conceded prerogative of Christ, prevents pride,
prevents anything but shame. Must the lecherous
forgive the malicious? the slothful the arrogant?
it seems no less. But not, surely, without a keener
sense of lechery or sloth, a renewed entreaty on his
own part, a confessed exchange of guilt. Not
perhaps, vocally, then and there; it is sometimes a
solecism to intrude one's own sins, though hardly to
remember them secretly.

"The falling out of faithful friends renewing is
of love"; the old poem has a deeper sense than
perhaps it altogether meant. The word "faithful"
certainly has. The mutual operation is an operation
of "faith"; it is a further entering into "the substance of things hoped for," a further exhibition of
"the evidence of things not seen." It may be
objected that such operations, in many and many a
relationship of love, are purely "natural"; they
neither invoke, nor think of invoking, the supernatural world of which St. Paul was thinking. So;
but then the great goods do operate naturally. Where
there is love, there is Christ; where there is human
reconciliation, there is the Church. To say so is

not in any way to weaken the supernatural : where the consciousness of that exists, the power of the operation ought in every way to pierce deeper, to last longer, to live stronger, than in the natural. The invocation of Immanuel is at the root of all, and where the invocation is conscious the consciousness of love should be greater. " Ought " . . . " should " . . . it is staringly obvious that in our present age it does not. The children of this world are even now in that other wiser than the children of light. And indeed for many of us it is the natural passion of love rather than the supernatural principle which directs and encourages us. This is well enough ; it is more than well ; so long as we intend to pursue the natural into the more-than-natural of which it is a part. The real distinction between Christians and non-Christians is here, as always, something very like the risk of hell. He who professes a supernatural validity for his virtuous acts must follow them out into that whole validity. He who professes only nature may be rewarded with the best of nature, perhaps with more than nature ; he who professes more than nature, if he does not practise it, may be left with neither. " Unto him that hath shall be given ; from him that hath not shall be taken away even that which he seemeth to have."

It is in relation to the next heading that the dependence of the natural on the supernatural can be again raised.

(iii) Things which cannot be forgiven. The phrase is only humanly true, and (everything considered) it is perhaps not even that. It would be dangerous to say that there is any princely goodness of which the human spirit is not capable; its original derivation beats in it still, and its divine kinship moves still in brain and blood. A perfection of pardon is not only a Christian dream. But it is, if not only, yet certainly, a Christian doctrine. Whether a pagan ought to forgive all injuries may depend on his own knowledge of spirit, on his "inner light." But it depends on no such unsure thing in a Christian; it depends on the will of Christ and the doctrine of the Church. The Christian has no doubt of his duty, though he may have every difficulty in fulfilling it. He is not, in that, very different from the faithful of other great religions; the Buddhist is a recipient of the same spiritual command. The difference between them, in that, is of another order. Forgiveness of all injuries is demanded of the Christian because of the nature of our Lord, and it is demanded entirely. The phrase "things that cannot be forgiven" is therefore to him intellectually meaningless. But it may in fact mean a good deal all the same. It is true that few of us are, fortunately, in a position to understand that meaning; no injuries of which the forgiveness seems unbelievable have ever been done us. But probably there are at the present moment more persons alive in Europe than for many generations to whom such injuries have been done. The forgiveness of the poor—even if a casual and pagan pardon; say, rather, the lack of resentment in the poor—we have had always with us, little though we have cared to understand it. But the massacres, the tortures, and the slavery, which have appeared in Europe of late have impressed themselves upon us. In the ruined houses of Rotterdam—or indeed of England—

among the oppressed thousands of Poland, there are those to which the phrase " things that cannot be forgiven " has a fearful meaning. Must they nevertheless be forgiven ? they must. Must vengeance, must even resentment, be put off ? it must. There is certainly a distinction between the desire for private vengeance and the execution of public justice. But there is no excuse for concealing private vengeance under the disguise of public justice. The establishment of tribunals to impose penalties for breach of treaty-agreements is, I suppose, possible ; how much more, if anything, may be either possible or desirable we need not here discuss. It would have nothing to do with its main theme ; and indeed of that main theme Rotterdam and Poland are only contemporary and spectacular examples, chosen for convenience. The injury done to many in that kind of war is greater than the injury done to one in private, but the result, from a Christian point of view, cannot be other. That must be, everywhere and always, the renewal of love. But in such a state as we are now considering, that renewal of love means little less than heroic sanctity. It is upon such heroic sanctities that the Church depends—depends in the sense that they are its rule, its energy, and its great examples. It is less likely, when the hurt is so deep, that there will be any request for forgiveness. The deeper the injury, the less inclined the evildoer is to ask, even to desire, that the sin may be forgiven— perhaps the less able. Remorse rather than repentance—with all that repentance means—is likely to exist ; there is already present the possibility of that kind of half-anger, half-anguish which is too easily built up into a continued wickedness, a separate hell.

The depth of vengeance on one side ; on the other, at best remorse, at worst persistence in injury—can these be turned into the reconciliation of love ? It is at least in such states of all but everlasting conflict that the Church expects the coming of peace, and that she demands, on the side of the injured, the heroic sanctity of pardon, or the interior preparation for it. In itself it may not properly exist until an opportunity is given it by the request ; it cannot be mutual till then ; therefore it cannot, in itself, *be* till then. But the whole passion of it must be there, waiting for the second's opportunity ; the spirit waiting for the letter, without which it cannot perfectly be. And here again it is to be maintained that, even in such difficult moments, the double responsibility of guilt enters ; sinner to sinner. Heroic sanctity is required perhaps to forgive, but *not* to forgive is ordinary sin. There is no alternative ; the greatness of the injury cannot supply that. It becomes—an excuse ? no, a temptation : the greater the injury, the greater the temptation ; the more excusable the sin, the no less sin.

It was said at the beginning of this book that it was impossible to write such a book ; and besides the impossibility of the theme, here is a side impossibility. Can any writer lay down such rules, for himself and for others—especially for others ? No ; and yet without those rules, without that appalling diagram of integrity, there can be no understanding, however small, of the nature of the interchange of love. For on the achievement in the extreme all depends. The courtesies of our first division, the intimacies of the second, spring only from the truth that the fact of forgiveness is absolute. Immanuel, by his existence in flesh, by his victimisation, by his life as forgiveness and by his proclamation of forgiveness, showed it as absolute. In doctrine and in action, the Church maintains the fact.

There are two footnotes, as it were, which should be added to the consideration of all three divisions. The first might be called the Rule of the Second Step. In matters of forgiveness, as in all other virtues (and some vices) the first step is comparatively simple compared to the second. Hell is always waiting for the rebound. The only prevention of the rebound is perseverance. The first moment of forgiveness is nearly always confused with other things—with affection, with delight, with honour, with pride, with love of power; some good, some bad, all distracting. It will happen, often enough, that the forgiveness is rather an emanation of these things than a power in itself. But then, directly afterwards, the good elements will withdraw themselves, and leave the reconciliation to its own serious energy; and if that energy is too weak, it will break; but it will not break alone, for the affection and the joy will be hurt too. Or else the evil elements, the pride and the sense of power, will dominate the reconciliation, and it will become egotistical and a false illusion of the good. Even the light courtesies and settings-aside of our first division need sometimes a second shrug: nothing is achieved at once.

> The horse is taught his manage, and no star
> Of wildest course but treads back his own steps;

> For the spent hurricane the air provides
> As fierce a successor ; the tide retreats
> But to return out of its hiding-place
> In the great deep ; all things have second birth.

The virtues, however wild their course, have to tread
back their own steps ; they have, young and innocent,
to be taught their manage. They have to learn to
be always ready when they are called on ; so, they
may in time, but only in time, be ready without the
calling ; their obedience to time and place in us sets
them there outside those conditions in the end :
" servitude and freedom are one and inter-changeable."

It is in relation to this management that the second
footnote may be useful : a footnote on recollection.
There are two methods of reconciliation : that which
remembers the injury in love and that which forgets
the injury in love. It is a delicate technique of pardon
which can distinguish and (without self-consciousness)
use either. Either may be desirable here and now,
though there can, of course, be no question which is
finally desirable and even necessary to the existence
of the Blessed City. There (its architect told us and
all its architecture maintains) all things are to be
known. We had better not forget it ; but even so,
" he that believeth shall not make haste." Oblivion
—say, perfect seclusion of the injury in God—is often
here a safer means. It is often likely that to remember
the injury would lead only to some opposite injury.
Even the best-intentioned Christians are not always
at ease in these sublime states. The mutual act of
forgiveness can, too often and too quickly, become a
single memory of the sin ; the single memory a
monstrous interior repetition of recollection ; the

monstrosity a boredom; the boredom a burden. Or, worse, the sense of superiority is too easily involved. We may say and think we have forgiven and then find we have not; or, worse again, think we have forgiven, and in that self-deception *never* find that we have not; we may die supposing ourselves to be kindly and self-pleasingly and virtuously reconciled—" And then will I profess unto them, I never knew you; depart from me, ye that work iniquity." But also we may in fact have forgiven—say, half-forgiven; and the pardon is thought to free the pardoner to every claim and compel the pardoned to every obedience. " Such," wrote Blake,

> Such is the Forgiveness of the Gods, the Moral Virtues of the
> Heathen, whose tender Mercies are Cruelty. But Jehovah's Salvation
> Is without Money and without Price, in the Continual Forgiveness of Sins,
> In the Perpetual Mutual Sacrifice in Great Eternity : for behold,
> There is none that liveth and sinneth not.

If it is forbidden to us to demand as a condition of our forgiveness any promise that the offence shall not be repeated, if when he conceded to us the declaration of reconciled love, God retained that condition to himself alone, how much more is it forbidden us to make any other claims, to expect an extra kindness, to ask for an extra indulgence. And how all but impossible to avoid ! Forgiving or forgiven, we can claim nothing, at the same time that we have, in God, a right to claim everything. Conceding the permission to promulgate, he conceded also the right to demand ;

in the Church such things happen. In sacramental
confession itself it is the priest who (conditions
fulfilled) cannot refuse absolution. Nor we forgiveness ; the sinner has all the advantages, as the just
son of the prodigal's father felt. But, so admitting,
we can slide into an evil mutuality : how easy to claim
consideration in return ; or if not to claim, at least
to expect ; or if not to expect, at least to feel we have
a right to—somewhere, somehow, *some* right ! Alas,
none but what our injurer, of free choice, gives us.
Otherwise, the mutuality itself becomes diseased ; it
grows corrupt with the dreadful stench of the old man
on the new way. To forget the sin is the safer
method.

Yet oblivion too has its dangers. The beauty of
the joyous and mutual interchange is bound to dwindle
a little if the occasion is put aside ; that is, between
lovers. And in those other more austere instances,
where love exists not as a strong and conscious
affection, but only as a deliberate act of the will—
in Rotterdam and Poland, say—even there, though
the soul can live from the wound of the heart, yet it is
perhaps less easy to learn to do so if the hurt is put
aside. Our derivation, our nourishment, is both
from our sorrows and from our joys ; it is so obvious,
and so harsh and lengthy, a business to find it there.
Say, Forget ; and add, But do not say Forget. Love
must carry itself beautifully ; it must have style. It
may seem absurd, in such high matters, to use so
common a literary term, and yet there is hardly any
word so useful. Style, in literature, is an individual
thing. *Le style, c'est l'homme même*—style is the
man himself, said the French maxim. Considering

what men are, it need not be pressed too far. Yeats indeed declared that a poet's work was often the antitype of his individual nature; he quoted Keats and Dante as examples. But in religion the problem hardly arises; in religion we are dealing with "the man himself" and there can be no separation. His style is his particular manner of courtesy; his lack of style is his lack of courtesy. It may be sedate or glorious, distant or intimate, firm or even flamboyant. Only, if it exists at all, and to the level at which it exists, it will not be insincere or partial. A purity of virtue will do much; it cannot, in any one case, do all. What is needed in every case, in every virtue, in every act of every virtue, is that all purities of intention should be precisely there. Pardon is perhaps the act in which all are most needed; it is apt to grow false if any are missing; it is quite certain not, then or thereafter, to have its proper joy. It gathers up within itself all the powers of love, because in fact it is love—chaste with the glowing chastity of the Divine Son. Chastity is the spirit of which courtesy is the letter; the spirit waits for the letter and the letter for the spirit; both together are love— love in knowledge, which is the only kind of love with which the Christian Church has, finally, any concern.

It would sound absurd to say that pardon itself has, on earth and between men and women, to be pardoned. Yet some kind of occasional meditation on this might not be unwise. "They feel most injured who have done the wrong"; and even if they repent and ask for forgiveness, they quite frequently begin to feel the forgiveness as an injury

when they have it. It is not easy to be forgiven;
certainly not to continue in the knowledge of being
forgiven. Only the princeliest souls can bear it
naturally for long; only the holiest supernaturally—
by which word is meant there not the pardon of God
for man, but the pardon of man for man in the Church.
There will be something selfish in the pardon; that,
at least, will be resented, if nothing more—improperly
resented, no doubt, but then it is itself an impropriety.
Our very forgiveness is an opportunity for us to be
forgiven—by God, of course, but also, and with more
tardiness, on our side and his, by our neighbour.
We were both sinners, we were both guilty—yes,
originally; but also we are both sinners and guilty
in the very act of penitence and pardon. Let it rest;
it is the very promise of life.

Such then is the relationship which is to be
attempted among the redeemed; which is, by virtue
of something else, to be achieved. The union of all
citizens of the City is not to leave out any facts.
Everything that has ever happened is to be a part of it,
so far as men are strong enough to bear it; the holier
the stronger. Everything that has ever happened
is an act of love or an act against love. Acts of love
unite the City; acts against love disunite. But of
this disunity it is necessary that we should not be too
quickly aware. The Lady Julian laid down a great
maxim when she said: " here was I learned that I
should see my own sin, and not other men's sins,
but if it may be for comfort and help of mine even-
Christians." The earthly courtesy which we discussed under the first of the three headings above is
a heavenly courtesy also. It is opposed to courtesy

in all its degrees that we should be too quick to cast
out the mote.

At the same time not even the greatest courtesy is
blind.   Love itself, as we know from Love itself, is
not blind.   If the mote in our neighbour's eye leads
him to murder another neighbour, we may presumably
notice it.   We are permitted to remark it when his
mote leads him to take away our coat, though we are
not then to insist on pulling it out ; we are, on the
contrary, to offer our cloak also.   It has been said a
hundred times that on those principles no organised
State could exist.   It is clear also that it is precisely
on those principles that the Church is intended to
exist, and does indeed exist ; at least it has no others.

The transfiguration of the earthly State into the
heavenly City is a work of the Holy Ghost.   The
word *transfiguration* there is apt ; it is a change of
diagram.   It does not involve, as the Manichæans do
vainly talk, a putting-off of the natural body, but it
does involve that natural body itself becoming accus-
tomed to a whole new set of laws—at first as commands, then as habits, last as instincts.   It has often
been pointed out that we use the word " law "
ambiguously ; that the " laws " of the Decalogue are
not the same thing as the " laws " of movement.
The alteration of the one into the other, individually
and generally, is the work of the Holy Spirit in the
Church.   It is an age-long work, and it has to be
done individually—even the general work has to be
done individually.   Efforts have been made—not too
successfully—to set up a Christian republic, a kind
of Christian anarchy, in which the secular State with
its laws and penalties should not exist.   It is not

merely from the greed or tyranny of the higher
ecclesiastics that the Church has so often felt uneasy
with even the most admirable State. The State, as
it were, longs to stand still; but the Church cannot
stand still. Her very name is speed; her Mind is set
always on virtues so great, on modes of living so
intense, that we cannot begin to imagine them. The
most elementary images of them are repulsive to us—
except at rare moments, and even then we are not
sure. Can we order all our affairs by instincts we
hardly begin to feel? to assert it and to deny it is
alike dangerous. Must we, for example, consent
that men, other men, shall be killed and maimed?
The answer to that is simple—we must. We may
do it by ourselves inflicting death and torment on
others (by bombs or however), or we may do it by
abandoning others to death and torment (in concen-
tration camps or wherever), but one way or the other
we have to consent by our mere acts. To call the
one war and the other peace does not help. This—
whichever it is—is certainly, in part, the result of
what we do. Is there any direction? Even to quote
" Thou shalt not kill " does not finally help, for we
have been taught that consciously to abandon men
to death is, in fact, to kill. To hate is to kill; to
kill is to kill; and to leave to be killed is to kill;
yes, though (like the lawyer in the Gospel) we do not
know who our neighbour is. There are wars to
which that does not apply; there are wars to which
it does. Such is the dilemma in which we find ourselves; and then what happens to forgiveness?

I have taken the most extreme example; but the
root dilemma is common enough. It is a dilemma in

which any man existing in an organised State is continually involved. Capital punishment, the whole penal law, the instability of the poor, a hundred social evils, are all part of it. To disagree with this and that no more helps us—or very little more—than to agree. While we remain part of the State we are involved in its life. Disagreeing leaves us where we were; we might as well disagree with the Fall, as no doubt most of us do. We cannot, so far, escape the nature of man, the original and awful co-inherence of man with man in which we were created. Certainly we must follow whichever path our conscience, under the authority of the Church, indicates; we must disagree with one and agree with one as we are instructed. But the moral burden is the same both ways.

What then are we to say, in this matter of forgiveness, about the State, if anything? especially, if such a thing can indeed exist, about the Christian State? Morally, of course, in the Christian State, where its members were all Christians, the matter would be simple in essence, though perhaps complex in operation. The courts would operate in a parallel order to the confessionals—only the confessions would be public. But that would certainly involve repentance on the part of the guilty. Whether in a profoundly Christian State it would be possible for the Church to produce a Guild of those who would vicariously bear the legal penalties on the part of the confessed criminals, even perhaps to the death penalty itself, if that were still imposed, is but a dream. Yet only by operations that once seemed no less of dreams has the Church reached its own present self-consciousness

—by devotions not dissimilar, powers not otherwise
practised. We do well to dream such things as long
as our dreams are in accord with the great Christian
vision. This is only another example of substitution,
upon which our Lord created the original universe,
and which he afterwards reintroduced in his own awful
Person as the basis of his redeemed world. Pardon
itself is an example of it ; the injured bears the trouble
of another's sin ; he who is forgiven receives the
freedom of another's love.

We shall have certainly to remake the State before
such things can be ; humanly speaking, we shall have
almost to remake the Church. But then we can never
quite talk of the Church " humanly speaking," and
the State we shall have to remake anyhow if it is to
last and succeed even naturally. The bounty of the
spirit then would be its freedom : our poverty can
only rise into that bounty by the practice of such
freedom as is found in a speed of giving and taking
forgiveness.

" The State's function," it has been said, " is
inherently ambiguous, and in some ways resembles
that of the Law in St. Paul's theology." [1] In the
matter of the secular law that ambiguity is mostly to
be discerned in the inevitable use of penalties. Punish-
ments, under the State, are either retributive or
reformatory. But either way they have to be enforced ;
they are put into operation by the decision and force
of the magistrates very much against the will of the
guilty. It is at least a question whether this, though
our only method, is not from the fundamental
Christian point of view, a false method. The chief

[1] *Christianity and Justice.* Canon O. C. Quick.

use of punishment in the State is to frighten the majority of citizens from behaving as they wish to behave, and as a minority do behave. But penance in the Church is not of this nature, nor is it retributive nor reformatory. It is much more in the nature of something undertaken, as a " satisfaction ", by the guilty and repentant person ; it is, that is to say, *desired*. The idea of that state which is called " purgatory " is not different. That certainly is purging, is reformatory ; but it is not entirely without the notion of compensation. The mountain of purgatory, wrote Dante, " shakes when some soul feels herself cleansed, and free to rise and mount. . . . Of that cleansing the will makes proof, which seizing the soul with surprise avails it to fly. It wills indeed earlier, but is not then free from that desire which the divine justice, against the will, sets as once towards sin, so now to the torment." The will to reach God is counteracted by the desire for the compensation of sin. But this is in the pardoned souls ; they are pardoned before they are in purgatory ; it is why they are in purgatory.

This flame towards both pardon and punishment is the mark then of the elect soul. It has its parallels in lower spheres. Lent, it has been said, is no such unjoyous season ; many a mortal lover, guilty of some offence, sighs for a penalty ; Shakespeare, as we saw, sealed it in Angelo—

> Immediate sentence then, and sequent death,
> Is all the grace I beg.

In such states penalties may be pronounced by authority ; they are invoked by the subject. The submissive is not passive only ; it is on fire with love; it hastens to experience the great balance of sin and punishment—the words separate too much what becomes a unity. But in the State punishment is bound to seem, at least partly, self-preservation. The community penalises offenders in order that it may itself live. It is not so in happier states; there, it may be said, punishment is love-preservation, and only self-inflicted. It was in relation to sin and pain that the Lady Julian said : " All shall be well, and all shall be well, and all manner of thing shall be well." Certainly in small things this can be seen; it is in the greater that it is difficult It is true that the same Lady said that all our life was penance, and perhaps the burden of life might be eased if it were taken that way. " A kind soul hath no hell but sin."

All this belongs to the place of division. But it points to the place of union. Forgiveness is the way to the state of union and first appreciation of the state of union. It is so that it is seen (to return to Shakespeare) in those concluding scenes of the plays which, more than many religious books, make the great human reconcilement credible. In that poetry it remains, as do so many of the experienced mysteries, a wholly human thing. It has been said of Shakespeare that he wrote the whole supernatural life in terms of the natural, and it is true that he is the great protagonist of natural life without apparent need— humanly speaking—of the supernatural. It was a divine gift to us; he remains for ever a rebuke to the arrogant supernaturalists; they try and annex him, but it will not serve. He may or he may not have been religious in his personal life; he is not, when all is said, even when what has here been said about

Cymbeline is said, religious in his poetry. But if anything of this nature could be deduced from his poetry, the one thing that could be deduced would be that man's human nature was made on the same principles as his supernatural. He is, in that sense, as necessary to check the excesses of the disciples of Dante as Dante is to check the excesses of his disciples. Either without the other is incomplete ; and it is not perhaps altogether by chance that Imogen and Beatrice are both the instruments and orators of pardon.

VII. FORGIVENESS AND RECONCILIATION

THE distinction, however, between the state of union to which forgiveness is a means and the opposite state is more extremely expressed in two other writers. The first of them is that admirable but heretical poet William Blake.[1] Forgiveness plays a great part both in the shorter poems and in those which go by the name of the *Prophetic Books*, especially the longest of them, called *Jerusalem*. This poem, like the other *Prophetic Books*, is concerned with the loves and wars, the destruction and salvation of great super-human beings. These beings pass from one kind of existence to another ; from a world of life to a world of death, and again to a world of life. It is true we cannot be very much interested in those great forms themselves ; they are not sufficiently clear for us to know or distinguish them, except after very careful study. But this is not so much incompetence on Blake's part as one might unwisely suppose. What he thought mattered was not " individuals " but " states " ; it was these states of being which he desired to define and declare, and individuals in his verse—even his own giant individuals—are only there to reveal the states of being in which they exist.

[1] I call Blake heretical for various reasons which cannot here be discussed. But I do so with some hesitation, since the explorations of his work which have been so far made have mostly been in the manner he denounced—by detached intellectual analysis. What might be found could a better method be discovered I do not think we know.

Poetically, this was no doubt a fault or at least a misfortune. The Divine Man in *Jerusalem* declares

> I go forth to create
> States to deliver Individuals evermore. Amen.

It cannot very well be done in verse, for it is only, on the whole, through the individuals that we know the states to which they belong. But it is true, on the other hand, that this way of thinking is, within proper limits, of great moral use to us. We normally tend to think of ourselves as *doing* something—as forgiving, as loving, as believing. Such a method of thought is perhaps all of which we are capable. But it is, as it were, wholly a doctrine of " works " ; the old hymn was not unjustified—

> Lay thy deadly doing down ;
> Doing ends in death.

The life of " faith " is preferable ; " faith " is the name given to an operation by which we are to become— become what ? become the Reconciliation. This does not rule out the necessity of what was said before about acts ; say, Do, and add, But do not do.

This passion of becoming was a great part of Blake's verse ; his figures labour with it. For our present purpose the two opposite states which he described are " vengeance " and " forgiveness." It might be argued that he too much ignores that idea of justice which is the root and effort of the State—or, not to confuse the word with two uses, let us say the Republic. The word Republic is, as everyone knows, derived from *res publica*, the public or common thing ; and it is precisely this common thing which has been in question. It is this, and not the individual soul,

which Christendom has taught us is, under the name of
the Christ-in-the-Church, Christ the City,
> the Eternal Vision, the Divine Similitude,
> In loves and tears of brothers, sisters, sons, fathers, and friends,
> Which if Man ceases to behold, he ceases to exist.
> . . . Our wars are wars of life and wounds of love,
> With intellectual spears and long winged arrows of thought.

We may or may not suffer from exterior things ; from
this interior thing we must all suffer—or almost all.
It is certainly possible that a few holy souls may have
been born already so disposed to sanctity that their
effort is natural and their growth instinctive ; they
move happily into goodness, and their regeneration
seems to have been one with their generation ; but
even they may have suffered more than they chose or
indeed were able to communicate. Their wounds
were hidden ; their sensitiveness bled privately ; they
appeased the rage of their companions in their own
quietude, and no one has done more than envy a
celsitude more painful than anyone knew. But for
the rest of us, the " wounds of love " mean a sudden
or a lingering death. The second death itself is indeed
but a choice in time ; if we prefer it before our
natural death, we are taught that it may be salvation ;
if after, that it may be eternal loss. The death of our
Lord introduced that choice. He who died in his
natural life brought into our natural life the possibility
of the choice of a supernatural death and therefore of a
supernatural life ; this is the life of faith.

> Wouldst thou love one who never died
> For thee, or ever die for one who had not died for thee ?
> And if God dieth not for Man, and giveth not himself
> Eternally for Man, Man could not exist ; for Man is Love
> As God is Love ; every kindness to another is a little Death
> In the Divine Image, nor can Man exist but by Brotherhood.

" Man is Love." I do not remember the divine epigram elsewhere. It is this which is the original part of all our life ; to divide it into natural and supernatural is a schism inevitable to us, but an inevitability only as a means to unite or disunite the common, the public thing. It is in our most private hearts that the Republic is established, but our private hearts can force themselves out of the Republic. We can refuse the maternity of Love, the protectorate of Grace : intolerable and too certain concession ! and then ?

> Hark ! and Record the terrible wonder, that the Punisher
> Mingles with his Victim's Spectre, enslavèd and tormented
> To him whom he has murder'd, bound in vengeance and
> enmity.
> Shudder not, but Write, and the hand of God will assist
> you.

The Sinner is forever justified ? no ; perhaps Blake was indeed heretical. Certainly the Republic is ambiguous, but the humanitarian terror of punishment will not be more than a Precursor, a St. John Baptist there. It is the fashion nowadays among many Christians to sneer at humanitarianism and liberalism (in the political sense), and this is natural because of the undue trust that has been reposed in them. But " the lights of nature and faith," wrote John Donne, " are subordinate John Baptists to Christ " ; humanitarianism is a formula of prophecy. Pity is still half a pagan virtue ; compassion a Christian. To forgive is indeed compassion, the suffering with another. To refuse to forgive is to refuse that other as himself or herself ; it is to prefer the spectre of him, and to prefer a spectre is to be for ever lost.

    All things are so constructed
And builded by the Divine hand that the sinner shall always
    escape ;
And he who takes vengeance alone is the criminal of Providence.
O Albion ! If thou takest vengeance, if thou revengest thy
    wrongs,
Thou art for ever lost ! What can I do to hinder the Sons
Of Albion from taking vengeance or how shall I them persuade?[1]

To say that the sinner shall always escape is a rash
definition. Our Lord did not say so. But he did
say that even the collection of our just human debts
was a very dangerous business ; he did say that we
were to pray to be forgiven *as*—precisely *as*—we
forgive ; he did say that the debts forgiven us reduced
to nonsense the debts owed to us. It is not therefore
to read the New Testament too rashly to see in it
rather more than a suggestion that, as far as we
humanly are concerned, the sinner will always escape.
The Church may blame ; it does not condemn—at
most it does but relegate the sinner to the Mercy of
God. The Republic may condemn ; it must not
blame—the judge has no business to do more than
pronounce a sentence. We are not yet—perhaps
in this world we shall never be—in that " state " when
the judges themselves may descend to be substitutes

[1] The figure called Albion in *Jerusalem* is said by the best commentators
(Messrs. Sloss and Wallis, in the Clarendon Press edition of the *Prophetic
Books*) to be a symbol of " the true relation of Time and Space with
Eternity," and so on ; and this is no doubt true. But it is also true that
the name stands, as it always has, for England, and this the commentators
allow. We do the poem less than justice if we read it, so to say," unpa-
triotically " ; it is a great spiritual appeal to and demand on England, and
the names of the English geography which fill it are not there by accident.
England itself is summoned to be a true relation of Time and Space with
Eternity. I have allowed Blake's possible heresy on the nature of Justice ;
it is the more reason for recollecting that that heresy recalls us to orthodox
Love. " Man is Love " is the maxim, and no one knew better than Blake
what an agony Man finds it.

for the condemned and to endure in their own persons the sentences they impose. But something like this is already the habit of the Church, for the Church mystically shares the vicarious sufferings of Christ. " The state of the punisher is eternal death." In the Church this is so, for in the Church he who takes vengeance is indeed already lost ; he is outside the Church, " outside which is no salvation " ; he is outside the City, where as St. John saw, are dogs and sorcerers and whoremongers, " and whoever liveth and maketh a lie." In the Church there is no punishment except when it is invoked and as long as it is invoked ; there is no punishment except through and because of pardon. There indeed the holy soul, aware at once of pardon and celestial vengeance, may sigh : " Both ! both ! "—too far beyond our vision to be more than momently comprehensible, and only at moments desirable. But it has been declared that the scars of Christ, the wounds of Love, are glorious in heaven ; and the justice of God glorifies the scars of Man who is also Love. The alternative ?

Instead of the Mutual Forgiveness, the Minute Particulars, I see
Pits of bitumen ever burning, artificial riches of the Canaanite
Like Lakes of liquid lead ; instead of heavenly Chapels, built
By our dear Lord, I see Worlds crusted with snows and ice.
I see a Wicker Idol woven round Jerusalem's children. I see
The Canaanite, the Amalekite, the Moabite, the Egyptian . .
Driven on the Void in incoherent despair into Non Entity.

Blake put the same vision more positively and more simply in one of the shorter poems :

> Thus through all eternity
> I forgive you, you forgive me :
> As our dear Redeemer said :
> This the Wine and this the Bread.

The orthodox Christian need not reject that quatrain.
If our Lord was indeed the very Person of forgiveness,
then certainly it is the very passion of forgiveness
which is communicated in the Eucharist; it is a
mutuality between God and man which is also
expressed between man and man. To feed on that
with a grudge or a resentment present in the brain,
or still lingering in the blood below the brain, is to
reject the divine Food that is swallowed; it is not
only to set schism between the body and the soul
but literally in the body itself. All things are finally
worked out in the body; all mysteries are there
manifested, even if still as mysteries. It is the only
crucible of the great experiment; its innocent, even
if debased, purity endures the most difficult trans-
mutations of the soul.

All this has reference to definite injuries definitely
inflicted. But there is more. Since the Fall we have
been subjected to pains, illnesses, and distresses whose
source is beyond our knowledge. Physical agonies,
caused by this and the other physical crisis, afflict us.
If these, as has been held, are the result of sin, then
they are the result of sinners : sin does not, for us,
exist without sinners. But since, for all practical
purposes, we do not know those sinners, then, for
practical purposes, they do not exist. They may be
ancestral or contemporaneous ; they may indeed be
our ignorant selves. The state of forgiveness must
cover these ; that is, a reconciliation, a love, must
cover them. We must forgive the evils we suffer
because of the dreadful co-inherence of all mankind,
even if we do not know who inflicts them ; and we
must be prepared to be forgiven when we discover,

knowing wholly and wholly known, the results of our own sin. To dwell on this is superfluous. When we are able to begin to forgive the known, we shall not have very much difficulty in forgiving the unknown; at least there we can believe there was no deliberate malice. True, but there was undeliberate carelessness. There was also our own sinful corruption which certainly infects humanity, somewhere, somehow, with the pain which is its inevitable accompaniment—which is, indeed, its very identity. The whole state of forgiveness must be whole; it is a state of being into which we grow and not a series of acts which we exercise, though (to repeat) we must exercise those acts in faith. Say, Do not do; and add, And then do. The supernatural is the birth of action in the death of action.

> O point of mutual forgiveness between enemies,
> Birthplace of the Lamb of God incomprehensible!

It was worth remembering Blake. But beyond Blake lies the Lady Julian of Norwich. Few, if any, of the English have written so greatly of pardon as she. She has been quoted already, and it is no part of this book's purpose to rewrite journalistically what she wrote celestially. But on the other hand no one can write a word of the absorption of human activities into that final Glory which the Church declares without remembering his august predecessor; and no book on such a subject ought to close without remembering the final Glory. The Atonement is the name given to an operation; an operation beyond our comprehension, but not beyond our attention; an operation by which everything—even hell—was made a part of that final Glory. The Atonement made possible the forgiveness of sins; or at least made it possible after the best manner. It enabled sin to be fully sin, and it fully counteracted sin. The maniacal obsession of selfishness in which, both necessarily and voluntarily, we live, was nowhere arbitrarily destroyed. I do not say that we do not wish it had pleased God to destroy it; of course, we do, even (many of us) at the small cost of destroying us with it. The penance of our life is too heavy. But in fact he neither forbore to create because we were about to sin nor ceased to sustain when we had begun to sin. It is the choice of a God, not of a man; we should have been less harsh. We should not have created because we could not have endured; we could not have willed; we could not have loved. It is the choice of a God, not of a man.

" This place is prison and this life is penance; and in the remedy he willeth that we rejoice. The remedy is that our Lord is with us, keeping and leading into the fulness of joy." The joy is to be complete and universal; even (mystically) hell is to be part of that joy. St. John saw wisely when he saw for a moment the smoke of the torment going up for ever and ever before the Lamb and before his angels, though that is impossible for any of us to understand and live : that is a Glory we cannot and ought not to endure. But at least, whatever " the smoke of their torment " means, it means something which the glorious company of heaven serenely tolerate, though only the glorious company; we need not be premature. There are things which can only be borne in the farther heavens, as Dante saw when Beatrice refused to smile at him in the nearer because he could not bear the smile. The mystery of unforgiven sin is one of these, and the knowledge of how this also is (if it exists) an element in the eternal joy. It is in every way wiser and better for us to have no part in it here that we may not need to have part in it hereafter. At the very least, if we condemn ourselves to have part in it, we shall have refused for ever the interchange of pardon. Whatever hell is, that interchange by definition it is not.

It is certainly now a part of the mystery to know what the relation may be between those who have been injured and, refusing to forgive, are cut off in hell, and those who have injured and repenting are assumed into heaven. Is it possible to be the occasion, by a committed wrong, of provoking that terrible refusal to forgive, and yet oneself to be in joy? Only the divine reassurance that nothing and no one can be the *cause* of sin except the unrepenting and unforgiving self could be then sufficient to content us. That reassurance will, no doubt, be sufficient; the least movement of Omnipotent Love within. But not to need the reassurance would be better; it would be better not to be compelled to sigh " O felix culpa " there; better to be, there as here, only the occasion of " fair love and fear and knowledge and holy hope." That is not altogether our choice; the avoidance of injuries, nothing else, is. But it will not be better to be known in heaven as a cause of injuries, forgiven or unforgiven, than of none.

Unforgiven sin then is beyond our guess. Forgiven sin, under the Protection, is not; it is forgiven sin that it remains to consider as an element in the

Glory. The unusual greatness of the Lady Julian is the two extremes which her book contains on the matter of sin. No one better understood the binding and harrowing nature of sin than she ; no one dared a loftier vision of its final transfiguration. What she said of that is contained in the 38th chapter of the *Revelations of Divine Love*. It runs :

" Also God shewed that sin shall be no shame to man, but worship. For right as to every sin is answering a pain by truth, right so for every sin, to the same soul is given a bliss by love : right as diverse sins are punished with diverse pains after that they be grievous, right so shall they be rewarded with diverse joys in Heaven after that they have been painful and sorrowful to the soul in earth. For the soul that shall come to Heaven is precious to God, and the place so worshipful that the goodness of God suffereth never that soul to sin that shall come there but which sin shall be rewarded ; and it is made known without end, and blissfully restored by overpassing worship."

" A pain by truth . . . a bliss by love," " Man is love." " God is Love." These, in the reverse order —or recurring rather in antiphonal order through the whole spiral of the heavenly stair—are the steps which lead to the knowledge of the new life. All is in the end a question of how we choose to know. Man at the time of the Fall, and continuously and voluntarily since, insisted on knowing good and evil ; that is, good *as* evil (since there was nothing but the good to know, the evil could only lie in the manner of knowing). The power had been conceded to him, did he choose to exercise it ; he did. There remained but one question of reconciliation : could the evil be wholly known as the means of good ? How that was effected is the subject of another volume in this series.[1] The effect was that man was victim as well as sinner ; and if man would know himself as the victim of his own sin—a triumphant or a defiant, but always a sacrificial—victim of sin, then it should be conceded to him to know the endured evil as good : not certainly the original good, for that could not be, but another, a new, good : " a pain by truth, a bliss by love."

The Lady's phrase is one that holds the heart and holds it either way. The pain by truth is the exclusion of sin from the City ; the bliss by love is the inclusion. In the old Jewish tradition, sin had been secluded into the secret knowledge of God alone. God had been said to have " forgotten " it : it was no longer to be part of the relationship of the soul with God. It is true that this is still a fact of the spiritual life. " I must," wrote Kierkegaard, " have faith that God in forgiving has forgotten what guilt there is . . . in thinking of God I must think that he has forgotten it, and so learn to dare to forget it myself in forgiveness." That state corresponds to the old Covenant, the Covenant of the simple exterior sacrifice. It is permitted ; it is even commanded ; we are not to remember our guilt.

Say then, Forget ; but add, Do not forget. With the rending of the veil and the entrance of the single High Priest into the state of the Holy of Holies (the perfect re-entry, as it were, into himself), the secluded knowledge was to be shared. In God it was hidden,

---

[1] *The Doctrine of the Atonement.* L. Spencer Thornton.

but then like all things in him it was a hidden joy.
With our entry into that renewed knowledge, it was
and is to be a joy to us also : a pain by truth, a bliss
by love.   Forgiveness is the knowing of it so.   To
call it only remembrance is futile ; the act, the sin
itself exists in him, as all things exist in him. The
exclusion of the sin from himself (were that possible)
must unimaginably exist in him.   But he would not
be content with that, nor would he have us be.   That
which must be excluded by justice must be included
by grace.   The sentence in which, more than in
most, our most courteous Lord exhibited at once his
freedom and his servitude was uttered at the point
of the opening of the Holy of Holies.   " Thinkest
thou I cannot now pray to my Father, and he shall
presently give me more than twelve legions of angels ?
but how then shall the scriptures be fulfilled, that
thus it must be ? "   Yet the scriptures were only there
because he had already decreed that thus it must be.
He could—or the Temptation means nothing—have
improperly evaded ; he could—or his sentence is
blasphemy—have properly avoided ; but he had
decreed that he would do neither.   He as Man would
forgive *thus*, because men also should not merely
be forgiven but also, in every corner of their natures,
forgive.

For the Atonement, like many other great, though
lesser, resolutions, is physical as well as spiritual—to
use once more that fatal intellectual dichotomy which
has done so much harm to Christendom.   It is, say
rather, carried out in the blood as well as the soul ;
the final seal of all things in this creation of our Lord
God's is physical ; it was, as was said at the beginning,

his very purpose in it. The forgiveness of sins, therefore, is a physical thing; that it certainly must be so before it is fully operative in every way is shown by the many times when the best intentions of our minds are overthrown by the revolt of our nerves. They are probably not as many as those when our minds quite steadily decline, in spite often of the witness of the flesh, to forgive or to ensure forgiveness. The flesh continually testifies, after its own manner, to the good. Our bodies are innocent compared to our souls, and their guiltiness is but that which they are compelled to borrow from the fallen will.

" By the fall," wrote William Law, " of our first father we have lost our first glorious bodies, that eternal, celestial flesh and blood which had as truly the nature of paradise and Heaven in it as our present bodies have the nature, mortality and corruption of this world in them : if, therefore, we are to be redeemed there is an absolute necessity that our souls be clothed again with this first paradisaical or heavenly flesh and blood, or we can never enter into the Kingdom of God. Now this is the reason why the Scriptures speak so particularly, so frequently, and so emphatically of the powerful blood of Christ, of the great benefit it is to us, of its redeeming, quickening, life-giving virtue ; it is because our first life or heavenly flesh and blood is born again in us, or derived again into us from this blood of Christ.

" Our blessed Lord, who died for us, had not only that outward flesh and blood, which He received from the Virgin Mary, and which died upon the Cross, but He had also a holy humanity of heavenly flesh and blood veiled under it, which was appointed by God to quicken, generate, and bring forth from itself such a holy offspring of immortal flesh and blood as Adam the first should have brought forth before his fall."

It was this heavenly humanity which forgave ; say, he forgave in his flesh, and therefore his very flesh forgave. As God, he could, no doubt, have forgiven—it is but to repeat from another angle what was said just now ; all the masters of that doctrine sound it together ; what without the Incarnation he could not have done—what, had he (*per impossibile*) after the Fall rejected the Incarnation, he could not have done—would have been to forgive as Man. " When Adam fell, God's Son fell "—not in the sense of sin but of distress—" because of the rightful one-ing which had been made in heaven God's Son might not be disparted from Adam. For by Adam I understand All-Man." It is therefore that the Eucharist is also that forgiveness of his flesh, and that we literally feed on forgiveness. Otherwise our now so-charged bodies would not have laboured with that vocation which, more than we suppose, is their own, however exacerbated they are with it. They are sometimes in revolt because our bodies are physically aware of the co-inherence with other bodies which our mental pickings and choosings reject. For—to quote the Lady Julian again—" Kind "—that is, Nature—" and Grace are of one accord : for Grace is of God, as Kind is of God : he is two in manner of working and one in love ; and neither of these worketh without other : nor may they be disparted."

What has blame outside the Glory of God has

worship within the Glory, provided that the blame can bring itself to come into the Glory. In the *Paradiso* of Dante a similar doctrine is laid down. In the third heaven Cunizza di Romano says to him "Joyously now do I grant indulgence to myself for the occasion of my fate here"; that is, she blessedly pardons herself for her being no higher or holier in heaven, taking delight in God's will; for in heaven "joy brings brightness"; and a few lines later the soul of Folco of Marseilles says the same thing: "Here we do not repent; we smile; not at the sin which does not come again to mind, but at the Worth that orders and provides . . . the Good which turns the world below into that which is above." Beyond that sphere, Dante says in a tremendous metaphor, colour ceases; the redeemed spirits are seen by their light alone.

That extreme effort to express the lofty (but not unfleshed) diagram of redemption should not detain us too long. Its value to us is that it restores us again to facts and not to what we feel about facts: it is to acts that we must return, for it is in acts that the Glory of God exists among us. It is permitted to us to be its occasions, but mostly here by faith. The splendour of it is not always obvious, nor the brightness of the joy. It is, again, permitted to us to encourage the joy; it is indeed commanded. But though the command is primary in itself, it is secondary in relation to the other commanded virtues. Chastity is before it, and truthfulness (that is, accuracy), and industry, and the duties of magnificence; and love, and therefore forgiveness. It is better to know it in joy, but it is still more im-

portant to know it, forgiving or forgiven. Either
way there are depths within depths. For a proper
forgiveness is so full a matter of the spirit that it leads
to the very centre of the Union. It is an exchange
of hearts. To forgive another involves, sooner or
later, so full an understanding of the injury, and of
its cause, that in some sense we ourselves have committed the injury; we are that which injures ourselves. And to be this we must very greatly have
got out of ourselves; and this is the means and seal
of the Church. The Church consists only of those
who have so gone out of themselves or are going or
desire to go out of themselves. The little word
" as " in the Lord's Prayer is the measurement of the
distance gone. Its final reach is to the Union; the
inGodding of man.

It is in relation to the inGodding that the clause
in the Apostles' Creed stands as one of the definitions
of eternity. The last paragraph is almost a description of the heavenly City of the Apocalypse. " I
believe in the Holy Ghost " is the foundation; " the
Holy Catholic Church " is the streets and markets,
the great co-inherence of souls; " the Communion
of Saints, the Forgiveness of Sins, the Resurrection
of the Body and the Life Everlasting " are the four
enclosing walls; and yet that metaphor is too remote,
for all are but four titles for the same co-inherence of
relationship. The Communion of Saints involves
the resurrection of all the past, and therefore the
forgiveness of sins. The resurrection involves forgiveness and communion. But the forgiveness is
the necessity of all. Where love is fate, this is fate.

VIII. THE PRESENT TIME

THERE lies now in many minds the general consideration of our relation to our present enemies. This problem, for those who feel it, is involved, of course, in all the preceding pages ; it has here and there been specifically alluded to. I do not feel myself in the best position to press it further, since, except for that inconvenience, loss, separation, and distress in which we are all involved, I have not so far suffered any direct disaster on account of the war ; that is, on account of my country's enemies. What I have suffered I might easily have suffered anyhow. Just as every death which is now died too soon must have been died in the end, and could not then be avoided, so our present unhappiness might for any and each of us have come had there been no war, or something very much like it. We do not avoid misery by avoiding *this* misery ; it is always the present misery which is unbearable, and existence, but for that, might, we feel, have been almost happy. It is false ; our suffering

> is permanent, obscure, and dark
> and hath the nature of infinity.

And our enemies, or the great majority of them, know it as well as we.

To press guilt upon them therefore is, to begin with, unwise ; we are all caught in the same trap. To begin therefore to forgive the present German

Government or indeed the Germans for our financial loss or our personal separation is for most of us nonsense; it is as difficult to forgive as to indict a nation. Without a direct sense of present personal injury by a particular person or persons there can hardly be any question of forgiveness.

But, it will be said, there are those who have directly suffered. There is also the sense of offence against morals—the treaty-breaking and the massacres. It is presumably the thought of those two problems which causes Mr. Churchill to refer to Herr Hitler as " that bad man." One must distinguish between the rhetorical force of the phrase and its literal meaning. The rhetorical force is of the greatest value to us at the present time, and may, of course, be entirely justified. It comes to us with a sense of the greatest sincerity, but that is only to say that Mr. Churchill is a superb rhetorician. In view of human history one can hardly believe that rhetoric necessarily implies sincerity. Men may be greatly moved by liars and knaves; indeed, we ourselves or many of us tend to assert that the Germans and Italians have precisely allowed themselves to be moved by liars and knaves. Our confidence in the Prime Minister need not be based on his style of public abuse. But the phrase " that bad man " does sum up a very general belief among the English people, Christians and non-Christians alike.

(1) To take the first problem first. It is clear that most of us cannot and ought not to start to forgive Herr Hitler on behalf of others. I say Herr Hitler for convenience of discussion, but the discussion applies equally to the German Government, or the

Nazi party, or indeed the whole German people, so
far as they are not covered by the modifications
proposed in the first paragraph of this section. It is
our enemies we are concerned with ; to say our
enemy singularly intensifies but does not alter the
discussion ; so long, at any rate, as we continue to
regard Herr Hitler as a responsible human being.
If we prefer to think him mad, we cannot hold him
as responsible, and the discussion ceases. You
cannot forgive a madman for you cannot be in proper
rational relation with him. You can, I suppose,
love him by such an act of goodwill as one might
exercise towards a cat or an angel. But his life (as
Wordsworth said) " is hid with Christ in God " ;
it is alien from us. There can be no mutuality.

One cannot then forgive on behalf of others. The
fact that many of us resent injuries on behalf of others
is generally a convenient way of indulging our resentments with an appearance of justice. Not always,
certainly ; there is such a thing as holy anger—" the
golden blazonries of Love irate "—mingled with
compassion. But holy anger is a very dangerous
thing indeed for any who are not saints to play about
with ; and I am not clear that it is very often found
in the saints. Supernatural indignation springs from
a supernatural root ; our business generally is to look
to the root. But if a facile resentment on behalf of
others is unwise, so is a facile pardon ; and other than
a facile pardon is a very deep matter. I am not saying
that it is impossible. It is to be admitted that a man
profoundly and permanently injured by a particular
German—say, a man who had been deliberately
crippled or a woman who had seen her husband
tortured—might feel himself unable to reach that

state of forgiveness which he conceived to be his duty.
He might therefore entreat anyone who loved him
to make an effort in that direction on his behalf.
Much may be done by a vicarious virtue, so only that
the original desire remains sincere and industrious.
A man may begin to be generous or devout or even
chaste in and through another, so long as his own
efforts to join himself with that virtue do not fail.
This certainly is the ground of our moral union with
Christ, but that union may itself be mediated from
him through others. This is part of the work of the
great contemplative Orders ; the invocation of saints
is the union of heaven and earth in the same labour ;
on earth the vision of romantic love is a vision of
virtue in another, and by the union of his devotion
with this a lover begins to follow the Way. There
are circles who are pledged to the consideration of
these mysteries, the exchange and union of intentions.
But such a vicarious beauty of achievement in forgiveness is a very different thing from the lamentable folly
of those who hurry, unharmed, to forgive or not to
forgive harm done to others. It is the direct purpose
of the injured alone that matters.

This attempt at direct forgiveness then means, as
has been said before, whether towards Herr Hitler
or the lowest creature in the Gestapo, an attempt at
direct goodwill, at the recollection and the knowledge
of the injury in love. It will be very hard ; it will
also be very dull. Forgiveness is not normally a
thrilling or an exciting thing. The metaphor which
our Lord used has a particular aptness—it is the taking
up, the carrying, the Cross, not the being crucified ;
it is the intolerable *weight* of the duty, and not its

agony, which defeats us—"the *weight* of glory." We do not (perhaps we need not) generally get as far as the Crucifixion. The direct injury, however lasting, is not to be allowed to deflect attention from doing the best thing at the moment ; the best thing, that is, for the Church, and therefore best for our enemy and best for ourselves. The best for the Church means the best in Christ. The conversion, where it is demanded, of the wild justice of revenge to the civil justice of the Divine City is the precise operation of the Holy Spirit towards Christ. All we need to do is to attend to the goodwill, to the civility ; the justice (in the personal relation) can be left to Christ. "Vengeance is mine ; I will repay, saith the Lord." It is perhaps desirable to notice that the repayment is not limited to our enemy. We shall be unfortunate if we forget the trespasses, the debts, which our enemies desire to repay with their wild justice and are content to leave to his promise. It is important that we should be ready to forgive the Germans ; it is not unimportant to recognise that many Germans (including Herr Hitler ? possibly ; we do not very well know) may feel that they have much to forgive us. Many reconciliations have unfortunately broken down because both parties have come prepared to forgive and unprepared to be forgiven. Instruction is as badly needed in this as in many other less vital things ; that holy light which we call humility has an exact power of illumination all its own.

(2) The problem of the general moral law is more difficult to define and not much more easy to practise. It was alluded to in Section VI., but what was said

there may perhaps be repeated. There is in existence
at the present time, so far as I know, no penal code
of international law. There are, that is to say, no
announced penalties, in the name of international
law, against national offenders. There are, of course,
the sanctions of the League of Nations; but they
were intended rather to discourage than to punish,
and they were intended to cease when they had served
their purpose of preventing or defeating aggression.
There is no legal way by which a breaker of treaties
can be brought before a tribunal; there is indeed no
tribunal for him to be brought before. We have not
been able to establish one because none of the nations
have found themselves able to trust the capacity of
other nations for just decision; there is no need to
look for worse motives; and indeed, considering
humanity, such a hesitation might be thought simple
caution. But that being so, there is, so far as I can
see, no way of punishing an offender, nor therefore
any method of formal acquittal or pardon. The
experience of the Versailles Treaty (not that I wish
to attack it as a whole) in which the Germans were
compelled to admit their guilt in 1914, was not
encouraging, nor, obviously, can be. It is (when all
modifications have been made) too much like confessions extracted under torture. It would be con-
ceivable, since murder is regarded as a criminal offence
in all States, to declare that it is a criminal offence as
between States, and that the beginning of military
operations without declaration of war, or the destruction of Rotterdam, were murder. It would be
possible to set up a tribunal to declare this, and then
to bring prisoners before it. But it would be a

retrospective decision, and some things (for example, the English bombing of German civilians—however justified or not) would put the tribunal in an ugly light. It would be, in the end, only a regularised and formal vengeance. We can take vengeance if we choose, but we must call it vengeance, for to take blood for blood without the specific contractual agreement of pre-ordained law is precisely vengeance.

There is certainly a sense in which execution might be done ; we might turn vengeance into sacrifice. It is dangerous, but it could be done. It puts almost too high—perhaps entirely too high—a responsibility on mortal men, but it is a responsibility we could accept if we chose. It might be declared that, though we had no precedent, we intended to establish a precedent. The new League of Nations (whatever form it may take) should not only rise out of the blood that has been shed in the war ; it should be definitely dedicated to the future with blood formally shed. If we are indeed victorious, and if our chief enemies fell into our hands, we might begin a new habit among the nations. We could not pretend we had any justification for it ; it would be a new thing. We should say, in effect : " We have no right to punish you for what you have done in the past. We admit it entirely. But we are determined that we will make it dangerous for men to do as you have done ; we will make it a matter of death. We shall sacrifice you to that new thing, though because it has not yet existed you cannot be guilty under it and must therefore be innocent of it. We shall therefore sacrifice you to our intentions ; and so awful a thing is this that it is an example, and the only worthy

example, of how mighty a thing we are trying to
do."

> This shall make
> Our purpose necessary and not envious,
> Which so appearing to the common eyes
> We shall be called purgers, not murderers.

But the purgation would be of our own hearts. The
execution of our enemy after that manner would be
an admission of our solidarity with him. We should
execute him not because he was different from us,
but because we were the same as he. The shedding
of that blood would be a pronunciation of a sentence
against us and our children if we denied or disobeyed
the law we had newly made. It would be an offering,
by the co-inherence of man, of the blood of the
co-inherence. " It is good," said Caiaphas, and spoke
a truth all civil governments have been compelled
to maintain—and ecclesiastical also; why else were
heretics condemned ?—" that one man should die
for the people." But then, humanly, the people
must know their blood one with his; they can only
thrive by his if they are willing that their own should
be shed; and they must know that so, but only so,
they do thrive by his. They must, in fact, answer,
according to their degree: " His blood be on us and
on our children."

It may be held—the question must be left to the
theologians—that this is impossible for Christians.
It would perhaps be too like a pagan sacrifice, too
much like Hiel who built up Jericho—" he laid the
foundation thereof in Abiram his firstborn, and set
up the gates thereof in his youngest son Segub," or
like the fable of Agamemnon who sacrificed his

daughter Iphigenia at the bidding of a god. It is said that she was caught away in a cloud as Isaac was saved by the interposition of a ram—the God of Israel maintained always (and in the end at his own expense) the atonement of blood. But whatever the result, whether the God was pitiful and forbore, or exact and accepted, or redeeming and substituted; whether Iphigenia was saved, or Abiram and Segub died, or Isaac was exchanged, yet human sacrifice has been forbidden to the new law, and by sacrifice is meant the dedicated ritual offering. To lose a thing by death or otherwise, even to kill a thing, is not necessarily to sacrifice it; the word is used too cheaply. It would have been supposed, not long ago, that human sacrifice as such, so ritual and dedicated, would have been impossible to our civilisation, but so much has returned that this too might return. Indeed, the only difference between this and the sacrifice of our enemy discussed above, is that whereas this is to a God, that is only to our best substitute for a God—our own solemn purposes for the future. Even so, it is greater than mere vengeance; it involves, for good or for evil, greater dreams of power. It is true that many people would be shocked at the thought of sacrifice who are not at all shocked at the idea of vengeance. They are perhaps right (or at least they would be if they had any idea of what they were thinking and saying). The problem is like that other—of adultery and divorce. Adultery is bad morals, but divorce is bad metaphysics. Bloody vengeance is a sin, but the bloody sacrifice is outrage.

It is, therefore, even for our future, our intention,

our safety (could it ensure them), forbidden to the
Church. Whether it is conceded outside the Church
is another matter; the Church, refusing it in one
sense, may allow it in another, as she does with
divorce. But she herself must not tamper with it.
Those who sincerely reject the Single Sacrifice may
perhaps be driven back on the many types of it, even
if—no, because the centrality of all the types is
unacknowledged. But belief in the Single must
refuse the multiplicity. The Rite of the shedding
of blood for atonement or for achievement, is accom-
plished. No other shedding of that kind is allowed,
unless God permits and enforces by physical states or
spiritual or both. Women's periods present the one;
the death of martyrs the other; the Eucharist both.
War and capital punishment are retained by the
Republic, and the Church concedes them to the
Republic—on the understanding that they are invoked
only by the guilty. His guilt is the invocation.
" A just war " means that the unjust party invokes
blood; it is his due, and he shall have it; the
unatoning blood. But the theologians must decide.

It seems then that there are, as regards our enemy,
four possibilities, both in the temper of our spirit
now and afterwards, and in action afterwards:
vengeance, justice, sacrifice, and forgiveness. Of
these, vengeance is in fact as difficult as any other,
for it is bound to be a limited vengeance, and that is
always a disappointing as well as an evil thing. It
is not, I suppose, intended to put all Germans (or
even a majority) to death, and if not then whoever
demands full vengeance will be disappointed. They
will have encouraged themselves to hate the survivors,

as the survivors will certainly hate them.   It is sometimes held that only by such a " lesson "—that is, by
the teaching of such doctrine—can our enemies be
taught.   This book is not the place to discuss it,
nor should be.   In so far as the idea of vengeance
enters, it is forbidden to the Christian to participate,
mentally or physically.

(2) Justice, in any legal sense, is impossible, for
there is no legal sense.   "The eye for an eye"
principle takes us straight back into vengeance ; any
other principle of penal justice demands prestatement,
and it has not been stated.   The enactment of retrospective international law would again take us into
vengeance (as a state of mind) or else into sacrifice.
That would depend on the state of mind. but either
way justice is impossible.[1]

(3) Sacrifice is possible to the non-Christian ; it
may be forbidden to the Christian.   Even for the
non-Christian it depends on an integrity of purpose,
on a depth of co-inherence, almost impossible to be
understood.   To kill the rulers of Germany, to
destroy Germany, is a vicarious action ; that is to say,
unless it is sacrifice it is murder, and if it is sacrifice,
it is sacrifice, to God or man, on our behalf.   The
blood is shed on behalf of our purpose and our life,
and the lives and purposes of our children ; if we
betray those purposes we become guilty of the blood ;

[1] I do not wish to seem to rule out such things as the immediate occupa-
tion or disarmament of the enemy countries, or the immediate display
there of military power and the formal result of defeat in war.   There
is a difference between the immediate control of an attack and the decision
on future relations.   It is however a dangerous period ; extension of
control, as we all know in many other and less widespread cases, always
has everything diplomatic, and generally has nothing decent, to be said
for it.

it becomes murder. It is a kind of image in human terms of the Sacrifice in Christian ; since there can now be no other deliberate image of that blood to Christians, that sacrifice is forbidden to Christians.

Vengeance then is forbidden ; sacrifice is forbidden ; justice is impossible : what remains ? the fourth choice ? forgiveness ? and how then forgiveness ?

It has been claimed here that forgiveness is a mutual act, but a disposition towards forgiveness is a necessary preliminary towards that act. The mutual act depends on two (or more) single dispositions ; we are not excused from our disposition because our enemies refuse to participate, nor is theirs less holy because we will not admit it. He who will claim the supernatural must claim it wholly ; its validity cannot be divided ; like the Blessed Trinity Itself it lives according to its proper complex method, but it altogether lives as a unity ; what we call the natural is but a part of the whole method. The mutual act of forgiveness is a holy thing ; the proper dispositions towards it, accepted or not accepted, remain holy. Who decides whether those dispositions are proper ? whether repentance is indeed repentance, or whether it is fear or greed or hate masquerading as repentance ? must we ? In fact we do because we must. No doubt in the end only God knows all, and we may forgive a hypocrite or reject a penitent. The danger of the last is the greater ; because our enemy may be penitent ? no, but because we ought to be. It is (let it be repeated) the guilty who forgives and not the innocent ; not perhaps the guilty in that one act, but guilty of how much else, of how much that led up to that act, guilty even in the very act of

mutual pardon—that is, of mutual reconciled love—
of how much of weakness, folly, reluctance, pride,
or greed. The guilty repents; the as greatly guilty
forgives; there is therefore but one maxim for both:
"make haste." It is one thing to be reasonably
intelligent, but quite another to be curiously inquisi-
tive or carefully watchful. We are part of him and
he of us; that is the centre; by his death there—his
death in that repentance—we live, and he by ours:
"dying each other's life, living each other's death."
It is all a question of whether he and we choose or
do not choose.

Both must wish, and will, to be a part of an act.
Do, and do not do. The union is in us becoming a
part of the act, not in the act being a part of us. But
if one of us does not wish to be? if we refuse co-
inherence? "Ephraim is joined to idols; let him
alone." If a man will be separate from the love
which is man's substance, he can; the ancient promise
holds: "I will choose their delusions." We had
better be very sure indeed that we have been injured
at the heart before we even think about forgiving;
we had better be very careful indeed that we are not
forgiving others' injuries, or no injuries, or merely
the inevitable pain of existence. Even our enemy is
not the universe, and we had better take care to forgive
him as himself (if we must) and not the universe in
him. But then we may pray to be in our degree made
a part of that act which is God and he and we—the
act we have only to be.

Whoever refuses . . . it is difficult to see what else
can be done except to leave him alone. If he shuts
himself out of the mortal co-inherence, or we; if he

shuts himself out of the act in which, more than any
other, the mortal co-inheres with the divine, or we ;
then that solitude is the answer. If it is he who
refuses, and we have been sincere in our goodwill,
then at least we are innocent there—if we have not
supposed ourselves to be innocent in anything else.
It is on the readiness and the speed with which we
move to become part of that act that all depends ;
so, corrupt, we may put on incorruption, and, mortal,
immortality. The reason why a thing possible
between men and women individually is almost
impossible communally is, obviously, that com-
munities are not individuals ; the analogy fails.
There are bound to be the innocent among the guilty
there ; there are misunderstandings which cannot be
explained, helplessnesses which ought not, on any
plea of justice or for any kind of claim, to be injured.

It is a lame conclusion ? a very lame conclusion.
Mortal ones are apt to be ; only divine conclusions
conclude. That the divine conclusion, being timeless,
" entered time " at a particular moment in time does
not seem to help much. The weight of glory is the
weight of the carrying the cross, " customary life's
exceeding injocundity." The labour towards our
enemy, individual or national, is a continual duty—
all Christians say so. Christian publicists indeed, in
that as in so many other things, are apt to sound as if
they thought they performed their moral duty merely
by teaching it ; it is easier to write a book repeating
that God is love than to think it ; it is easier, that is,
to say it publicly than to think it privately. Unfortunately, to be of any use, it has to be thought very
privately, and thought very hard. To be used

towards that thought is, after trying to think it ourselves, our chief business. It is the thought of the world which matters, but thought, like charity, begins at home. It has indeed been held that thought and charity were one; certainly charity is not so much a colour of thought as a particular kind of thought. I had almost said, of accurate thought, but then there is no other. Charity is not a delay in our usual mental habits; it is a change of mental habit; it is the restoration of accurate mental habit. This is everyone's business, for his friend's sake and his enemy's and his own. And if indeed we are all in danger of hell, then very much for his own.